CHINA 2020

China 2020

*How Western Business Can—and
Should—Influence Social and Political
Change in the Coming Decade*

Michael A. Santoro

Cornell University Press
Ithaca and London

First published 2009 by Cornell University Press

Printed in the United States of America

Library of Congress Cataloging-in-Publication Data

Santoro, Michael A.
    China 2020 : how western business can and should influence social and
political change in the coming decade / Michael A. Santoro.
        p. cm.
    Includes bibliographical references and index.
    ISBN 978-0-8014-4695-5 (cloth : alk. paper)
  1. China—Foreign economic relations.   2. China—Commercial
policy.   3. International business enterprises—China.   4. Investments,
Foreign—China.   5. Social responsibility of business—China.
6. Business ethics—China.   7. Social change—China—21st century.
8. Human rights—China.   9. China—Social conditions—21st century.
10. China—Politics and government—21st century.   I. Title.

    HF1604.S26 2009
    322'.30951—dc22

200850888

Cornell University Press strives to use environmentally responsible
suppliers and materials to the fullest extent possible in the publishing of
its books. Such materials include vegetable-based, low-VOC inks and
acid-free papers that are recycled, totally chlorine-free, or partly composed
of nonwood fibers. For further information, visit our website at www.
cornellpress.cornell.edu.

Cloth printing   10 9 8 7 6 5 4 3 2 1

Contents

PREFACE

Almost a decade has passed since I wrote another book—*Profits and Principles: Global Capitalism and Human Rights in China* (Cornell 2000)—on pretty much the same subject for the same publisher. So the reader naturally might wonder why I decided to write a second book and whether I have changed my mind about anything in the intervening years.

Profits and Principles came out when the United States was debating whether to admit China into the World Trade Organization (WTO). I had the privilege of testifying before the Finance Committee of the United States Senate on the human rights implications of China's entry into the WTO. Drawing on research in *Profits and Principles,* I argued that multinational corporations, foreign investment, and economic privatization were helping to move China toward greater democracy and human rights. Based at least in part on the premise that there was a connection between economic openness and political change, the United States approved China's WTO membership. This result irked many human rights activists, academics, politicians, and pundits who believed that using trade sanctions to punish China was the best way to promote human rights.

I began this book with the goal of testing whether evidence from the past decade supported the argument in *Profits and Principles* that economic openness was moving China toward greater democracy and human rights. Although the evidence did indeed point to significant political progress, the ultimate outcome remains far from certain. As my research progressed, I became more interested in understanding the forces that would help to shape social and political change in the next decade.

The potential outcomes for China in the next decade are widely divergent. It might continue to progress steadily toward greater democracy and respect for human rights. But it might as likely fall backward into an ever more authoritarian regime. Given that China is poised to move in one of two such polar opposite directions, it is no overstatement to suggest that the next decade will be one of the most important in the history of China, and, owing to China's global impact, the history of the modern world. This book describes various tectonic social and political struggles going on within China. As we shall see, the outcomes of these battles will depend on a number of powerful indigenous forces as well as the decisions and actions of individual Chinese citizens. The current global financial crisis—which has affected China far more significantly than most Westerners realize—has served to intensify and raise the stakes of these broad social and political tensions. The principal argument of this book is that Westerners can—and should—influence these developments.

This book is much more pointed in its criticism of Western business than is my earlier book. The "fair share" standard of corporate moral responsibility for human rights is the same one enunciated in *Profits and Principles*. I continue to believe that Western business is helping to unleash powerful forces of change in China. But when we look at the behavior of Western firms, it is clear that they are not doing their "fair share" and that there is much more they can and should do. Foreign companies have settled into a complacent partnership with the Chinese government. This is not morally acceptable. Nor is it in the long-term interest of business. My hope is that this book will shake up this complacency by shining a light on the faulty moral and strategic premises on which it rests.

This book also has a greater appreciation for the interdependence of what had been treated as two distinct kinds of questions in the first book and also in two hithertofore separate branches of scholarly debate. What will be the effect of economic reform and prosperity on political reform? How can companies operate with moral integrity and ethics in China? The book unifies those two fields of inquiry by demonstrating that the ethical behavior of multinational corporations will be a decisive factor in determining whether economic reform will lead to political reform.

Our collective understanding about what is going on within China has increased considerably since *Profits and Principles* was published. Many good books, scholarly and popular, have been written. Western press coverage of events within China is much more extensive. There are regular exchanges of tourists, students, and government officials. However, China's emergence as a global economic power has raised the stakes of mutual understanding exponentially. The gap between what we understand and what we need to understand has grown wider. The global financial meltdown has, moreover, changed the rules for China's future prosperity and for Western business interests in China. This book attempts to elucidate what forces will shape China and how Western business can influence that future. Western business executives hopefully will find both a moral and a practical guide for investing and doing business in China. It should also be of interest to politicians, policymakers, union leaders, and human rights activists who want to understand the potential extent and limits of Western influence on democracy and human rights. I hope, in particular, that *China 2020* will be useful to the new Obama administration as it struggles with the decades-long foreign policy puzzle of how to effectively and morally reconcile human rights with the other weighty concerns that complicate America's relationship with China.

One caveat I offered in my earlier book is worth reiterating. The methodology is interdisciplinary and practical. As a result, it risks offending purists in a number of fields, including Sinologists, moral philosophers, legal scholars, economists, political scientists, sociologists, and business journalists, to name the first that come to mind. Others who might regard this work as an intellectual impertinence include foreign affairs specialists, management scholars, and experts on cross-cultural interactions. I mean no offense or scholarly arrogance by blundering into these realms. The subject is very complex, and therefore I was required to draw from a wide array of fields. I am in some measure beholden to all these disciplines. It is impossible to do good interdisciplinary work unless one can rely on high quality disciplinary work.

When I refer to "Western" business, I mean to suggest firms based in Europe and the United States. Because of my background and network of contacts, most, though by no means all, of the firms I discuss are based in the United States. Nevertheless, I hope what I have to say resonates with Europeans and Canadians as well, despite the fact that some readers will very likely (with some justification) regard many of the premises and goals of this book as peculiarly American in character. (Apologies also to citizens of other South and North American countries for occasionally usurping the American name to refer only to the United States.)

I hope that this book will help to formulate a road map for mutual cooperation and respect between China and the West. The specter of another Westerner telling the Chinese how to run their country is, I'm certain, very tiresome if not downright offensive. Indeed, if the current financial crisis has taught us anything, it is that the West and China have been co-dependently pursuing an unsustainable economic model that married cheap, unaccountable Chinese manufacturing with Western consumerism and debt. As we look to the future, I argue that many of China's internal issues that in the past have been seen as contentious and divisive—for example, worker rights, product safety, and the rule of law—should be viewed as essential building blocks for the emergence of China as a global economic power. Finally, I sincerely hope that Chinese readers will regard this book as measured and reasonable. Although my criticisms are uncensored and unsparing, my motivation is not to tear down or disrespect China. In the almost two decades I have been traveling to China, I have developed great affection and admiration for its people, many of whom I count as good friends. I hope Chinese citizens will see that I write out of a genuine spirit of *chu yu ai xin,* that is, "being critical but out of a love of heart."

ACKNOWLEDGMENTS

For nearly two decades, I have been traveling to China every year to teach MBA students and Chinese managers and to conduct field research in factories and offices. In that time, I have discussed the matters in this book with hundreds of Western and Chinese businesspersons, academics, lawyers, diplomats, human rights advocates, workers, government officials, students, and others who gave generously of their time and insights. Although I cannot name all of them (nor, incidentally, would most of them wish to be named because of the sensitivity of the topics), I want to note my appreciation for the contributions they have made to my understanding.

I am grateful for the careful reading and comments of two anonymous reviewers. They made many penetrating criticisms that convinced me to fortify and rewrite parts of the manuscript, although perhaps not as much as they would have liked. I also want to thank my Rutgers colleagues—Wayne Eastman, Kevin Kolben, and David Bensman—for their helpful comments on various chapters. Chao C. Chen very patiently helped me to appreciate many subtle aspects of Chinese culture. Other colleagues, including Leonard Goodman, David Finegold, Mariana Spatareanu, Don McCabe, Mahmud Hassan, Lei Lei, Sharan Jagpal, dt olgilvie, Kelly Brantner, Cindy Jensen, Sharon Lydon, Abe Weiss, and Claudia Meer provided encouragement and support. In particular, I want to thank Dean Michael Cooper for valuing ethics in his vision of twenty-first-century business education. I am also very grateful that some years ago Karen Eggleston of Stanford's Shorenstein Asia-Pacific Research Center suggested that I meld my interests in China and the pharmaceutical industry.

I am especially fortunate to count as good friends a team of accomplished and talented journalists—Caitlin Liu, Cait Murphy, and Pamela Yatsko—each of whom read various chapters. Wendy Goldberg generously shared her deep knowledge of the Internet industry and offered valuable editing suggestions. Dorothee Baumann was an invaluable resource on current trends in corporate social responsibility.

Various chapters were presented over the years at meetings of the Society for Business Ethics, and a number of colleagues there made useful suggestions. I also want express my sincere appreciation to Prof. Stanley Lubman, the dean of Chinese legal studies in the West, for generously commenting on the rule of law chapter, though those who find fault with it should be comforted to know that he expressed abundant criticisms and reservations, and one should not presume that he agreed with any of it.

I gratefully acknowledge the able research assistance of Yulan Liang, Bharat Mohan, Stephanie A. Murray, Qiqi Wang, and Alexia Chan. The Aresty Research Center for Undergraduates, under the leadership of Justine Hernandez Levine, has provided funding for a number of talented Rutgers undergraduate research assistants. I also gratefully acknowledge the Rutgers Business School Research Resources Committee for several research and travel grants. My students at Rutgers deserve a special note of thanks for patiently helping me to work out many of my ideas as "works in progress."

Many good friends and family provided all manner of support and encouragement throughout the writing of this book. I can't name them all but among them are Salvatore and Diane Santoro, Jane Tse Barnet, Joe Ruggiero and Howard Marcus, Deb Hanna, Adam and Elizabeth Barker, Kate Becher, Brewer Stone, Monica and Mitchell Dolin, Liz Rubin, Tony James and Wanda McClain, Desiree and Tim Reiff, Danny Eldridge, Tom

Abrams, Lauren Abendshein, Gary Noble, Gretchen Worth, Mary Child, and Patty Cateura.

Finally, I want to express a special note of gratitude to the editorial staff of Cornell University Press and to my editor, Fran Benson, in particular. Fran's intellectual vision helped to shape this book. Her wit, joyful spirit, and unwavering confidence helped to sustain my drive to finish it.

CHINA 2020

1

BEYOND THE SHADOW OF TIANANMEN

The Role of Foreign Business in China's Uncertain Path to Democracy and Human Rights

When the Olympic cauldron rose into the night sky above Beijing's National Stadium on August 8, 2008, it marked a momentous step in China's emergence as a global power. The riveting spectacle, a combination of fireworks, high-tech wizardry and precisely choreographed routines executed by thousands of Chinese citizens was extravagant even by Olympic standards. When the elaborate ceremony was completed without a misstep, most ordinary Chinese people, some 1.3 billion of them, collectively exhaled—a sigh of relief mixed with nationalistic pride. With the Olympics, China's moment on the world stage had arrived. For two weeks, global attention was riveted on China, and China put on a spectacular show. Chinese athletes performed with distinction, accumulating more gold medals than any other nation. Outside the stadium, Beijing seemed transformed into a modern metropolis, with soaring skyscrapers, (almost) clear air, a prosperous workforce, and orderly traffic. Teary-eyed basketball star Yao Ming summed up the feelings of a nation when he declared that these Olympics were about "optimism and hope for the future." President Hu Jintao declared that the Olympics were "an opportunity not only for China but for the whole world" to "deepen mutual understanding." With these Olympic Games, China had truly put its best foot forward.

China's Olympic moment was especially poignant for millions of older Chinese who remembered that on October 1, 1949, less than ten miles directly south of the Olympic Stadium, Mao Zedong stood at the Gate of Heavenly Peace overlooking Tiananmen Square and declared that "the Chinese people have stood up." As he spoke from the exact spot where for centuries emperors had addressed their loyal subjects, every Chinese person knew what Mao meant. The founding of the People's Republic of China marked the end of the "century of shame" when this proud and ancient nation had been occupied by foreigners, first by Europeans starting in the nineteenth century and then by Japan during the Second World War. Now, nearly sixty years later, China was having its coming-out party. While there had certainly been significant setbacks—like the tens of millions who starved to death during Mao's disastrous economic folly of "the Great Leap Forward" in the late 1950s and the millions more who suffered extreme degradation, humiliation, forced labor, and physical abuse during the Cultural Revolution of the 1960s—these setbacks seemed rooted in a distant past as China basked in the glow of the Olympic torch.

Nearly three decades have passed since Deng Xiaoping declared that "to get rich is glorious." In that time, China has embraced free market economics, enjoying approximately 10 percent annual economic growth. Hundreds of millions of Chinese have been lifted out of poverty. Foreign investors are eager to invest billions to bet on the country's future. In 1997, China reacquired Hong Kong from the United Kingdom, ending another humiliating chapter in its history. The Olympics marked the strongest sign yet of China's power and prestige. In this shining moment, China could even dream of being reunited with Taiwan. What power, riches, and glory could lie ahead in the twenty-first, the Asian, the Chinese Century?

Although China's Olympic moment was domestically exhilarating, many Western observers had a decidedly different perspective; these negative images and attitudes could be termed the "Shadow of Tiananmen." Many Westerners still cannot forget the searing images of China from June 1989: students occupying Tiananmen Square and erecting the Goddess of Democracy; the same students and workers being slaughtered in the streets by People's Liberation Army soldiers; and a brave, solitary man defiantly standing in front of a column of rolling tanks. For many Westerners, the dark legacy of Tiananmen will always define China no matter how prosperous and powerful it becomes.

In the years leading up to the Olympic Games, the collective concept of the Shadow of Tiananmen permeated the Western media through a steady drumbeat of negative stories: lead paint in toys, environmental catastrophes, child labor scandals, Internet censorship, toxic toothpaste, crackdowns on human rights, deadly pet food, counterfeit medicine, and on and on. Seemingly every day one organization or another issued a formulaic press release about the Olympic torch "shining a light" on corruption, incompetence, or human rights violations. Much of the criticism about China is warranted—in its rush to the future, corners have been cut, which have resulted in numerous catastrophes—but the larger truth is that China has become the country that many in the West love to hate. In the Shadow of Tiananmen mirror, every negative media report only serves to confirm the view that China is a growing menace, run by a ruthless dictatorship that has little regard for its own people and which poses a grave threat to freedom, global safety, and public health.

Eventually, the Olympic torch itself, ostensibly a symbol of global unity, became for some a symbol of Chinese oppression. In Paris in March 2008, a French protester, upset over China's military crackdown in Tibet, climbed onto the balustrade of the Chinese embassy, tore down the Chinese flag, and unfurled a Tibetan flag. Later, another group of protesters broke through security forces and attacked Jin Jing, a wheelchair athlete, as she carried the torch through the streets of Paris. The Olympic torch was briefly extinguished, and security forces had to rescue Jin Jing from an unruly mob.

The reaction in China was swift and virulent. As news of the incident circulated on the Internet, anger and nationalistic pride boiled over. Protesters threatened to boycott French products and expressed their outrage at French-owned Carrefour department stores. The anger and resentment became so intense that the Chinese government soon took steps to tamp it down, including censoring related Internet discussions. Eventually, the president of the French Senate traveled to China to apologize to Jin Jing. On the other side, China, realizing that Carrefour employed forty thousand Chinese workers and that French investment in China amounted to billions, was also eager to move on. Jin Jing appeared on Chinese television to start a "China Smiles for the World" campaign, presenting a welcoming face to the world in anticipation of the Olympics.

China's Olympic moment was meant to herald its emergence as a global power. After the Olympic Games concluded, however, when the medals had been awarded and the closing ceremony ended, China's relationship with the West remained an uneasy one. Even the spectacular opening ceremony, which had engendered awe and pride among Chinese citizens, left many in the West perplexed and uncomfortable. Behind the overwhelming glitz, human spectacle, and technical wizardry, Zhang Yimou, the ceremony's impresario, had concocted a not so subtle ideological mélange clearly meant to explain and justify China to the world. Progress and openness were celebrated but so too were the sublimation of the individual to society and the hope for a "harmonious society" free of messy conflict or dissonance. Many Westerners viewing the spectacle looked on uneasily as goose-stepping People's Liberation Army soldiers raised the Olympic flag. China, which had cautioned foreigners to keep politics out of the Olympics, made its own political ideology the overwrought and self-absorbed centerpiece of its glittering welcome to the world.

The Shadow of Tiananmen proved to be so great that it continues to loom over China long after the Olympic flame has been extinguished. For many Chinese, conversely, the fact that so many in the rest of the world would not allow them to fully enjoy their Olympic moment tempered their pride and joy somewhat, and endures as a bitter and lingering resentment. After two weeks of athletic excellence and good will, China and the West returned to their complicated, perplexing, and often worrisome relationship.

In this book I focus on the cluster of social, economic, and political problems that constitute the Shadow of Tiananmen. As the title *China 2020* implies, the book looks forward. The Olympic moment has passed. So, too, have the twentieth anniversary of the Beijing Massacre, three decades of economic reform, and nearly a decade of China's membership in the World Trade Organization. China today is struggling to restructure its economic model to respond to a global financial meltdown. It's a good time to ask "what's next." This book is primarily addressed to those Westerners who would like to understand China's challenges and how they are likely to be solved—or not—in the next decade. The book is not simply descriptive or historical. It also considers moral and ethical questions stemming from China's increasing role as a world financial power: What role can, or should, foreigners play in helping to define and solve China's social problems? Do multinational companies have moral and ethical responsibilities within China other than maximizing profits? Although this book's intended audience is the West, it might also provide a basis for China to better understand the perspectives and concerns of foreigners and result in more constructive engagement with them.

China's Problems: From the Outside Looking In

The number and variety of concerns Westerners have about China is remarkable—from Tibet to Sudan, from human rights to environmental degradation, from Internet freedom to toy safety, from sweatshop labor to the development of a fair and modern legal system. The list is seemingly endless. It is worth noting, however, that foreigners have a very different set of priorities than do Chinese citizens. According to a 2008 Chinese Academy of Social Sciences "blue paper," the top concern of both urban and rural Chinese residents is the rising price of consumer goods, closely followed by growing income inequality and corruption.[1] A 2008 Pew Research Center Study corroborated these results. Only about 10 percent of Chinese citizens reported being very concerned about the environment and product safety, whereas nearly half were very concerned about inequality and corruption and over 70 percent about inflation.[2]

The disparity between foreign and domestic views of China's problems does not mean that the concerns of foreigners are illegitimate. One could, in fact, argue that the domestic list would be quite different if the researchers felt free to ask, and ordinary citizens were free to answer, questions about democracy and human rights. However, what is crucial to our understanding of modern China is that the concerns and priorities of foreigners are not necessarily shared by the Chinese people. Moreover, behind all of the problems that foreigners focus on, there are numerous pragmatic concerns and broad social problems, such as rural poverty, health care, and lack of coordination among central, provincial, and local governments, which have much greater impact on the day-to-day lives of Chinese citizens. This book considers the broad impacts of such indigenous forces as it analyzes a representative sample of the problems that most concern foreigners.

Why do so many foreigners have such strong opinions about China? Certainly, selfless humanitarianism is one important motivation. Westerners care about China because we see its government systematically and pervasively violating what we believe to be the most basic and fundamental human rights of Chinese citizens. We feel ambivalent about buying cheap Chinese imports because we worry that we are contributing to child labor abuses or the violation of workers' rights. We are concerned about multinational corporations that invest billions in China because we think they might be contributing to suppression of basic freedoms. We are horrified by corruption and lack of governmentally enforced safety measures that result in poisonous food, products, and medicine. We worry that corporate investment might be legitimating and enriching an authoritarian regime. We are appalled at China's heavy-handed repression of Tibetan and Uighur cultural and religious heritages.

Humanitarian concerns are not, however, the only reason Westerners care about what happens inside China; a good amount of self-interest is also at work. Because so many of our manufactured goods and, increasingly, our food and drugs come from there, China's health and safety problems have de facto become our health and safety problems. Sometimes our concerns are a blend of humanitarian concern and self-interest. We care about sweatshop workers—but we also want to protect our own factory jobs, and we hope that if we can get China to raise its labor standards we might be able to make Western manufacturing industries more competitive. Our concern for China's environment is also driven by the same kind of mixed motivations. We care about the many millions of villagers being displaced by the Three Gorges Dam and we worry about the toxic algae in Tai Lake in Jiangsu Province because we care about the health of Chinese citizens. But we also worry about the effect of China's rapidly growing carbon footprint on global warming. (China has surpassed the United States as the world's largest emitter of carbon dioxide [CO_2] and is responsible for two-thirds of the annual global growth in CO_2.)

A final set of concerns is about sharing global power with an illiberal, authoritarian government. The economic rise and heightened profile of a country with one-fifth of the world's population is bound to have a profound effect on the global world order. China is not only beginning to exercise significant influence in Southeast Asia; its economic power now extends to Africa and South America. It is one of the five permanent members of the United Nations Security Council. Many in the West believe that democracies, at least those that respect civil and political liberties, do not go to war with one another.[3] Hence, we worry that China will be a destabilizing presence, unless it evolves to the point where its government displays greater accountability to its citizens and respect for human rights.

The four subjects discussed in this book were selected as a representative sample of the broad array of foreigners' concerns about China. The sweatshop problem in chapter 2 primarily attracts global interest out of humanitarian concern, although a good deal of old-fashioned protectionism is also at work. In chapter 3 the discussion of pharmaceutical safety is about the negative externalities that Chinese manufacturing creates for consumers outside of China. Chapter 4 is about how China deals with Internet freedom, and chapter 5 provides a glimpse into the rule of law. The promise of Internet technology and the evolving rule of law may go a long way in signaling what kind of impact China is likely to have on the future of the global world order, and both subjects also involve fundamental human rights issues. The four topics I have chosen are meant to be representative of the broad range of subjects that have a combination of internal or external effects or which involve systemic issues. In each case I seek to illuminate how these problems are likely to unfold in the coming decade, as well as the critical role of foreigners. In chapter 6, I conclude by considering how the resolution of these and other issues, such as environmental sustainability, will impact China's economic and political development in the next decade.

From Inside Looking Out: Chinese Resentment of Foreign Criticism

As the furor over the Olympic torch protests illustrates, many Chinese people are weary of and even hostile to foreign criticism. In the past two decades there has been a gradual transition in China's collective attitude toward foreign criticism, from defensiveness to defiance. In the wake of the Beijing Massacre in 1989, there was a firestorm of global outrage. In November 1991, China's State Council issued a "white paper," *Human Rights in China,* defending the government's actions. The white paper made three basic contentions: (1) China must give priority to political stability and economic opportunities over political rights; (2) human rights fall within the purview of national sovereignty, and so foreigners should not meddle with China's internal affairs; and (3) human rights must be interpreted and implemented in accordance with China's distinctive cultural values and norms, which prioritize the needs of the group over that of the individual. The white paper concludes that "the right to subsistence is the most important of human rights, without which the other rights are out of the question."[4] In the two decades since the Beijing Massacre, these now-familiar arguments have formed the bedrock of China's defense against foreign criticism of its human rights record.

In contrast to the defensive posture outlined in the 1991 white paper, the Chinese response to the Olympic torch protests was not only defiant but also hostile. Fueling this virulence are decades of nationalist fervor deliberately cultivated by the Communist Party, through schools and state-controlled media, over issues ranging from human rights and territorial controversies with Japan to relations with Taiwan and Tibet. Before the founding of the People's Republic in 1949, China lived under foreign domination for nearly a century. Appeals to sovereignty and national pride thus have deep resonance for most Chinese, many of whom believe that foreign powers still conspire to keep their nation from its rightful place as a world power. The government has also used nationalism to divert attention from domestic issues. Political scientist David Shambaugh has observed that this "hyper-nationalism is also fueled by the deep feelings of discontent and resentment currently gripping large sectors of Chinese society—wage arrears, stagnant incomes, unemployment, inflation, corruption, severe class disparities, environmental deterioration, a moral vacuum and a deep sense of losing ground in China's Hobbesian economy."[5] This rising tide of nationalism will be a significant factor in China's foreign relations in the coming decade. In her book *China: Fragile Superpower,* Susan Shirk argues that the Communist Party's constant public emphasis on standing up to foreigners could end up painting the government into a corner, forcing it to be dangerously confrontational over issues such as Taiwan for fear of appearing weak to its own citizens.[6]

Lurking below the nationalist sentiments of ordinary Chinese citizens is a reservoir of resentment and hostility that has gradually grown in response to a constant barrage of negative images of China presented in the foreign media. What is perhaps most worrisome about this sentiment is that it is prevalent among younger, more affluent and educated citizens, even those with personal exposure to the West. A focus group among overseas Chinese conducted in the United States at the height of the fury over the Olympic torch revealed the depth of this growing resentment of Western media criticism.[7] One Chinese citizen educated in the United States and now working at an American investment bank stated that "the irresponsible illusion of China in most of the collective Westerner mind is primarily caused by the distortion from its media, the deeply-rooted prejudice against China in the past, the Cold-War mentality, the unease of watching China surpass other nations and emerge as a great power, the blindness of European or Western supremacy under the pretext of high morality and 'democracy'." When pressed, he admitted, "I feel saddened and angry about the media distortion. I feel angry because of the distortion of Western media controlled by some special interest group and some Western government with the intention of creating some instability in China to hinder the further development of the country." A young Chinese journalist visiting the United States for the first time thought that "Western countries have some misunderstanding of China because we are not developing as they planned and thought. We are not completely Westernized. Westerners like to measure China's development with their own values and experience, so that's why they don't understand some problems we are facing now and think we should just be like them. Also, China's rapid development certainly influenced some other countries' economy so they want us to pay back for that."[8] A college sophomore from China reflected that "the furor among Chinese population about the Western media distortion is beyond my expectations but, at the same time, understandable. Their misreporting and biased views made us realize that Chinese media are not the only ones that are 'brainwashing' people."[9]

Nationalistic sentiments run so high that it sometimes becomes dangerous for Chinese citizens to adopt a friendly or even conciliatory posture toward Western perspectives. One of the ugliest incidents emanating from the Olympic torch controversy involved Grace Wang, a twenty-year-old Chinese national who was a student at Duke University. When Wang tried to mediate between pro-Tibet and pro-China demonstrators at a rally, her picture was posted on the Internet in China. Bloggers and other online commentators called her a "traitor" and worse. Her family was harassed in her Chinese hometown. This kind of excessiveness worried even patriotic Chinese citizens. "Some irrational reactions committed by some Chinese against Grace Wang upset me a little," said one college freshman. "I am glad to see that Chinese people are concerned about their country, but it will be more favorable for us to have a more open mind for other opinions that are different from ours."[10] Another student expressed fear about the backlash and what it could portend: "I am scared, because it seems like the Cultural Revolution is back again within my friends and peers. The patriotism is too strong to let others to say no. Also, the Red patriotic activities overseas may let the Western society feel uneasy, because for so many years Red Communism is related to horror in people's mind. It would cause averseness toward overseas Chinese people. This may influence our life, since we are still studying in the Western world."[11]

The weariness and hostility felt by Chinese citizens when they are criticized presents a special challenge to a book that hopes to inform foreigners about how to think about China's problems and encourages businesspeople, union leaders, and others to do something about them. As has been noted, even the same "problems" look very different from a Chinese perspective. It is understandable why even a foreign executive comfortable operating in the Chinese cultural context would be reluctant to become involved in discussions about the country's internal challenges. The final chapter offers some suggestions on how to discuss such difficult issues.

Toward a Unified Theory of Economic Reform and Political Change: The Impact of Corporate Ethical Behavior

Since the late 1970s China has embarked on a steady course of economic reform. The three most fundamental elements of this "reform era" have been rural privatization, the consolidation and privatization of the state-owned industrial sector, and opening up to foreign investment. In the first phase, Deng Xiaoping dismantled the collective ownership and operation of farms and introduced a system of private ownership, which he called "household responsibility." The results were immediate and dramatic. Between 1978 and 1984, the output of China's three main crops— grain, cotton, and oil-producing crops—increased at annual rates of 4.8 percent, 7.7 percent, and 13.8 percent, respectively, as compared with average rates of increase of 2.4 percent, 1.0 percent, and 0.8 percent per year from 1952 to 1977. Just as dramatic as the agricultural production increases was the excess labor created by increases in efficiency. In the same period, between 1978 and 1984, the farming share of overall national employment declined from approximately 70 percent to 40 percent.[12] This in turn resulted in what will continue in the coming decade to be one of China's most vexing problems—the more than a hundred million workers who, no longer necessary on the farm, migrated across the country to urban areas and manufacturing hubs in search of jobs.

The second phase of the reform era was the consolidation and privatization of state-owned enterprises. In a painful process beginning in the early 1990s, China has all but completely dismantled the "iron rice bowl," one of the key institutional pillars of the Communist era. The metaphor of the iron rice bowl centered on the idea that the socialist state guaranteed housing, education, medical benefits, lifetime employment and retirement income, at least for urban factory workers. Factory workers during the Communist era were, after Communist Party bureaucrats, the economic and social elite of China. From 1985 to 2003, however, the state share of gross industrial output declined from approximately 78 percent to 38 percent. Over that same period, the percentage of all workers employed by state-owned enterprises declined from just under 14 percent to just over 6 percent.[13] As the privatization of the industrial sector and the dismantling of the "iron rice bowl" continue, China will face enormous challenges in providing its citizens with the social welfare benefits it once provided through the workplace.[14]

The third major element of the reform era has been a dramatic increase in foreign trade and investment, particularly after China's accession to the World Trade Organization in 2000. China now accounts for 12 percent of all global trade and rivals the United States in attracting foreign direct investment. With foreign exchange reserves of over $1 trillion, China has become the biggest holder of U.S. government debt.

The results of economic reform have been extraordinary. In addition to averaging an extraordinary 10 percent annual growth over three decades, according to the World Bank more than two hundred million Chinese have been lifted out of absolute poverty. In urban and coastal areas, a new middle class is enjoying a lifestyle unimaginable under Communism, complete with cars, kitchen appliances, cell phones, and trendy clothes. The benefits of this growth, however, have been unevenly distributed. There are still hundreds of millions of Chinese citizens mired in rural poverty. Laid-off workers in state-owned enterprises unable to adjust to the market economy are living a nightmare of insecurity and poverty they never could have imagined in the days of the "iron rice bowl." Nevertheless, China's economic success story has made it the envy of the developing world and an indispensable market for global trade. Rare is the company that doesn't have a "China strategy" for manufacturing or sales. Economics have turned Red China white hot for trade and investment.

This book unifies what have heretofore been two distinct questions that have accompanied China's economic rise. One is an empirical question: What will be the effect of economic reform and prosperity on political reform? The second is a moral question: How can foreign companies operate with moral integrity and ethics in China? This book unifies those two fields of inquiry by demonstrating that the ethics of multinational corporations constitute a key factor in determining whether economic reform and prosperity will bring political reform. Economic reform is, in fact, having a profound effect on social and political change. But the pace and trajectory of change in China crucially depend on the extent to which multinational corporations act with courage, vision, and moral integrity.

The uncertain relationship of China's economic rise to its prospects for greater democracy and human rights has created sharp controversy among policymakers and academics. When the U.S. Congress was debating China's accession to the WTO in the spring and summer of 2000, a significant part of the debate concerned the effect of WTO membership on its prospects for democracy and human rights. To be sure, raw economic interests and a full-scale lobbying effort by the business community were mostly responsible for the vote favoring China's admission. For many in Congress, however, and for many Americans, the decision to support expanded economic ties with China depended on the hope that economic engagement would spur improvements to China's human rights practices and prospects for democracy. Not everyone shared this rosy perspective. Many observers in the popular press argued that increasing economic ties with China would strengthen and legitimate the grip of a repressive regime.[15] Corporate executives, eager to do business with China, claimed somewhat self-servingly that economic engagement would lead ineluctably to greater freedoms and democracy for the Chinese people.[16]

Almost a decade later, the debate over the effect of economic engagement on democracy and human rights is far from settled. Broadly speaking, one can discern two schools of thought that might be termed the Optimists and the Pessimists. The Optimists tend to emphasize the positive impact of both domestic economic reforms and foreign direct investment on social and political change. For example, in his research on state-owned enterprises in the Shanghai area, the sociologist Doug Guthrie found that the emergence of the market economy increases the significance of price, quality, and service in commercial relations between companies and renders traditional *guanxi* (personal ties)-based market relationships "unimportant."[17] Another study, on highly paid urban workers and their foreign managers in Beijing and Shanghai, found that Western companies investing in China to build long-term market share (in contrast to companies attracted by low-wage manufacturing) influence "four sets of factors—economic prosperity, merit-based hiring practices, information-sharing and teamwork, and leadership values—that have an 'elective affinity' with human rights and democracy."[18]

While the Optimists emphasize that foreign investment and economic transformation engender social and political change, the Pessimists argue that economic reforms and foreign direct investment have strengthened the overwhelming power of the Chinese state to incorporate and control any incipient political change. The political scientist Mary Elizabeth Gallagher argues that the liberalization of foreign direct investment prior to political reforms "has led to a delay in political change by enhancing the capacity of the [Chinese Communist Party] to implement difficult reforms while maintaining a political monopoly."[19] Bruce J. Dickson, also a political scientist, paints a similarly gloomy picture of the willingness and capacity of "red capitalists" to effect political change, concluding that private Chinese entrepreneurs "do not seek autonomy but rather closer embeddedness with the state."[20]

So who is correct? In certain respects, both Optimists and Pessimists capture part of the truth. Anyone who has visited China in recent years can plainly see that economic reform is bringing about sweeping social change. Chinese citizens have opportunities to move from one job to another and to travel abroad. Many young women in the workforce have acquired economic freedom and autonomy, which enables them to exercise unprecedented choice in their personal lives and in their selection of marriage partners. Chinese citizens also have opportunities to communicate social and political opinions and even influence government actions to a degree unimaginable in the pre-reform era. Just as surely, however, the Chinese Communist Party (CCP) is moving deftly to preserve its power by attempting to channel, defuse, and control emerging economic and social forces. Will the CCP successfully maintain its monopolistic grip on power? Or will the social and cultural change engendered by economic reform make it impossible for the CCP to continue to dominate China? The outcome is far from historically determined. One of the principal themes of this book is that the next decade of China's history will be shaped more by human choices than by ironclad social and economic forces. Multinational corporations and other foreign actors—including nongovernmental organizations (NGOs) and international trade unions—will play a critical role in determining China's progress. The only question is whether that role will be positive or negative, and that will depend on the moral choices these foreign actors make.

A "Fair Share" Theory of Corporate Responsibility for Human Rights

In this book I argue that Western businesses have a moral responsibility to do considerably more than they are currently doing to advance labor rights, product safety, Internet freedom, and the rule of law in China. On the eve of the second decade of the twenty-first century, the idea that corporations have social responsibilities other than maximizing profits has become an increasingly accepted notion.[21] However, it is worth reflecting upon the philosophical foundations that underpin this notion.[22]

The moral argument for corporate social responsibility can be constructed from many philosophical premises. One useful approach is the "social contract."[23] Broadly speaking, the idea of a corporate social contract is based on the political social contract in the writings of John Locke, Jean-Jacques Rousseau, and Thomas Hobbes. The "social contract" is meant to signify the relationship of trust existing between corporations and society. The very existence of a corporation as a legal "person" is made possible by society. Society also enacts and enforces the legal norms and institutions that protect private property, the accumulation of capital, and profits. In return for what society makes possible for them, corporations are accountable to society. They have a "contractual" moral duty to operate in a manner that benefits society.

A corporation's moral responsibility for human rights is a particular instance of its duty to be socially responsible in its conduct. Human rights are rights of such importance that they impose correlative duties on actors beyond a nation's borders.[24] To call something a "human right" is to say that it imposes duties on others across national borders to honor that right. Human rights are moral rights. Human rights exist regardless of whether a particular national government in actuality protects those rights. The apartheid laws of South Africa vividly illustrate the idea that the law, customs, and mores of a country can lose their presumptive validity in cases where they conflict with human rights. It does not matter that the South African government passed legally binding apartheid laws; those laws were in conflict with the fundamental human right not to be discriminated against on the basis of race. This idea that individuals might have moral rights separate and distinct from those rights protected and promulgated by national laws puts human rights in tension with the absolute sovereignty of the nation-state in the international political order.[25]

Another essential aspect of human rights is that they impose correlative duties. At a minimum, a human right imposes a primary duty on every actor, absent some overriding moral justification or excuse, not to violate that right or to assist someone else in doing so. In certain circumstances, the existence of a human right also imposes a secondary duty on actors to take action to remedy the violation, even in cases in which those actors are not themselves directly involved. The Sullivan Principles for multinational corporations doing business in South Africa in the apartheid era involved precisely this sort of promotion of human rights. Companies adhering to the Sullivan Principles were expected not only to fulfill their primary duty to reject the practice of apartheid in their own operations. They were also expected to fulfill a secondary duty to work "to eliminate laws and customs that impede social, economic, and political justice."[26]

The claim that corporations should not participate in or assist others in the violation of human rights is relatively uncontroversial, though there are many gray areas in which it is not so clear whether or not corporations are being complicit. Moreover, such violations could under certain special circumstances potentially be justified or excused. Nevertheless, the very idea of a human *right* would be meaningless if it did not by definition imply that other actors, including corporations, had a correlative moral *duty* to avoid violating that right directly or indirectly.[27]

In considering whether corporations also have such a secondary duty to help ameliorate or remedy human rights violations perpetrated by others, three actor-specific fairness factors should be taken into account: (1) the relationship of the corporation to the human rights victims (the closer the relationship, the stronger the duty); (2) the potential effectiveness of the corporation in promoting human rights (the greater chance of being effective, the stronger the duty); and (3) the capacity of the corporation to withstand economic retaliation (the greater capacity to withstand retaliation, the stronger the duty).

In addition to these three criteria, another systemic fairness factor must be taken into account: The diversity of actors (all with their own actor-specific criteria) who might also owe human rights duties to the victims. Although moral responsibility for human rights belongs ultimately to individuals, it is most effectively discharged collectively. Acting collectively, individuals are able to accomplish much more than they can alone. Nation-states represent the collective will and interests of their citizens. Nation-states, in turn, collectively act through intergovernmental institutions such as the United Nations. In recent decades, NGOs such as Human Rights Watch and Amnesty International have become important channels for collective efforts to promote human rights. NGOs represent the collective will of a group of individuals, bypassing the nation-state system.

Multinational corporations are just one of several types of collective enterprises with significant powers and correlative human rights responsibilities. The importance of taking into account the duties owed by other actors is often insufficiently appreciated by those who seek to impose human rights duties on multinational corporations. What appears to be at work is a kind of "last man standing" phenomenon. Apart from a few international criminal courts specially convened to prosecute the most heinous of genocidal crimes, there is no international mechanism for enforcing human rights. The burden of enforcing human rights falls in a haphazard manner upon various international actors. When international institutions, such as the UN or individual nation-states, fail to remedy human rights violations, activists understandably turn to corporations. Multinational corporations do possess great power, wealth, and influence, and therefore they do have a responsibility to help to shoulder the burdens of enforcing human rights. It is, however, easy to overestimate their actual power and potential effectiveness.

The particular human rights duties of any one actor cannot be understood in isolation. The duties of each actor depend on the duties of other actors. All of these public, private, and nongovernmental actors have different strengths and weaknesses, or actor-specific criteria. In assessing how fair it is to ask multinational corporations to engage in the upholding and promotion of human rights, the systemic factor instructs us to consider the strengths and weaknesses of multinational corporations relative to those of other actors.

The "Fair Share" theory of corporate human rights responsibility can thus be summarized and applied in China as follows.[28] Corporations have a primary duty not to directly violate or assist others in violating human rights. Corporations may also have a secondary duty to attempt to remedy human rights violations in which they are not directly or indirectly complicit. This secondary duty depends on their relationship to the human rights victims, the potential impact their actions can have, and their ability to withstand the potential cost of retaliation by the Chinese government. This secondary duty also depends on the strengths and weaknesses of corporate actors relative to other collective actors, most notably national governments, intergovernmental organizations, and NGOs. There is no mathematical formula for weighing all of these criteria; only by taking these various criteria into account can we say that we are asking multinational corporations to do their "fair share" in honoring and promoting human rights in China. In the chapters that follow, these general "Fair Share" principles will be applied to various issues involving corporate responsibility for human rights in China.

The Crucial Decade: Looking Ahead to China 2020

China's next decade will be one of the most important in its long history, and how that history unfolds will impact the entire world. China is a nation where many basic values are in contention and its fundamental social and political institutions are in flux. What emerges from this cauldron of change and experimentation will truly shake the world.

Beyond its seemingly inevitable rise as a global economic and political power, what should we be looking at to understand the kind of nation China will become? From the outside, we in the West see many problems. How these problems will be resolved is far from certain because the problems themselves are extremely complex. This complexity is driven by China's combination of distinctive institutional, cultural, economic, and political factors. The path China will follow will be shaped by the courage and choices of both its political elites and ordinary people. Although the main roles in the drama will principally be performed by domestic actors, foreigners also have a crucial role to play.

The chapters that follow consider four specific issues: sweatshop labor, product safety, Internet freedom, and the rule of law. In each case, the degree to which the next decade of economic development will bring corresponding progress in democracy and human rights will depend at least in part on whether multinational corporations do their "fair share." The ethics of multinational corporations—and also other actors such as NGOs and labor unions—will help to determine whether (or not) economic reform and prosperity will lead to political reform.

At this critical juncture in China's history, many ordinary citizens are bravely using the legal system to advance their rights, pushing the boundaries of acceptable speech on the Internet and pressing for the rights of workers. Many of these citizens are in prison because of their courageous actions. To date, the foreign business community has been too afraid of jeopardizing both their profits and their continued presence in China to play as constructive a role as they might in China's development. Multinational corporations have rarely deviated even slightly from acting in their own narrowly perceived economic self-interest. They have settled into a complacent partnership with the Chinese government. Foreign business and investment have contributed to an extraordinary prosperity for the Chinese people. This prosperity, in turn, has unleashed many progressive social and political forces. But foreign companies can and should do more. This book is meant to challenge the foreign business community to behave with more courage and do its "fair share" to advance democracy and human rights in China. The argument for doing their "fair share" is a moral one. However, in this book I also make an economic argument: Foreign investment in China will never truly be secure unless it is embedded in a society where rights, including economic rights, are respected, where the government bureaucracy is effective in enforcing market regulations, and where a strong and independent rule of law protects the rights and economic interests of its citizens. Because it's the right thing to do and because it is in its economic interest, Western business in China can—and should—do more to influence social and political change in the coming decade.

2

The Clipboard, the Megaphone, and Socialist Characteristics

Pragmatic and Ideological Approaches to Solving China's Sweatshop Problem

One of the most common and evocative images of China is the sweatshop worker. Exploited and humiliated by her employer and oppressed by her own government, the Chinese worker commands an extraordinary amount of global attention and sympathy. Contributing to this attention is bit of old-fashioned protectionism and a belief that the low labor standards in China are responsible for the loss of blue-collar jobs in the West. Mostly, however, foreigners are concerned about the rights and well-being of the workers. Sweatshop labor is thus a quintessential example of an issue where criticism of China is primarily based on humanitarian concerns for Chinese citizens.

Low pay, forced overtime, child labor, and the inability to form independent trade unions are all issues that raise significant economic and moral issues. A long-standing and vigorous debate among economists questions whether raising the minimum wage helps workers or hurts them by discouraging investment and increasing unemployment.[1] Philosophers, too, have debated whether forcing someone to work overtime represents the kind of coercion that raises moral concerns or whether it is simply a morally acceptable condition of work.[2] These economic and moral controversies have informed a public policy debate about whether trade institutions and agreements such as the World Trade Organization and the North American Free Trade Agreement should contain provisions conditioning trade rights on adherence to certain minimal labor standards.[3]

Because so much of the world's low-wage production takes place in China, it has become a focal point for the antisweatshop movement. Labor rights campaigns led by international and regional nongovernmental organizations have fueled global outrage with a "bigger they are, the harder they fall" strategy focused on such well-known brand names as Wal-Mart and Dell. Activists have called on these companies to take responsibility for labor practices in their supply chain, allow independent monitoring of the factories of their subcontractors, and take tangible steps to assure worker representation and empowerment.

In response to the negative publicity heaped upon them by labor rights activists, many global brand-name companies have devised an elaborate and costly system dubbed "corporate social responsibility" (CSR).[4] They have hired consultants with clipboards to audit the factories of their subcontractors. A few companies that are more socially innovative are not simply monitoring existing conditions but also attempting to address the root causes of the problem by encouraging changes in management practices at the factory level. Often these efforts are undertaken in close cooperation with NGOs. Despite the efforts of brand-name companies to manage the labor issues in their supply chain, however, many in the NGO community have begun to question the fundamental premises of CSR. These activists argue that the CSR system as a whole has been too imperfectly administered and inadequate in scope to truly solve the sweatshop problem in China.

As the ideological drama between NGOs and global brands plays out, the Chinese government has attempted to remain relevant. Most significantly, the new Labor Contract Law came into effect in 2008, providing, at least on paper, worker protections that exceed those in the United States and even rival those in the labor-friendly European Union. In addition, the All China Federation of Trade Unions (ACFTU), under the direct control of the Communist Party, has stepped up recruitment, particularly among workers employed by foreign companies. The ACFTU characterizes itself as a union with "socialist characteristics," a nod to the Communist Party's account of economic reform consisting of "capital-ism with socialist characteristics." What this means in practice is that the ACFTU sees as its primary role being loyal to the Communist Party and helping the Party maintain civil stability; advancing worker interests is secondary and only within its broader mandate. Despite such ideological shackles, the ACFTU has actually enjoyed some pragmatic accomplish-ments, including succeeding at what heretofore has been unthinkable for the U.S. labor movement—creating a union at Wal-Mart.

In this chapter I consider the economic and social origins of China's "sweatshop problem." The "sweatshop problem" as discussed in this chap-ter concerns the rights of migrants working in the export sector, and as such it is a relatively small subset of larger labor rights issues in China. I emphasize this group because that is where foreigners have the most con-tacts with Chinese workers and where they have the most leverage and can make the greatest difference. Moreover, many of the problems and opportunities that face migrant workers in the export sector are highly correlated with those that face other private-sector laborers in China's manufacturing sector.

The "Other China": Supply-Side Origins of the Sweatshop Problem

What to the rest of the world is China's sweatshop problem is from a Chinese perspective an epiphenomenon reflective of a series of far broader and even more vexing national problems. This is not to say that worker-rights issues are not real and significant in their own right. Within the Chinese context, the global sweatshop problem is a manifestation of mas-sive poverty in most interior sections of the country, a growing inequality between rural and urban areas, and the plight of more than one hundred million young migrant workers from the countryside who have migrated without legal rights or a social safety net into the more prosperous urban and coastal areas.

Most tourists and businesspeople experience China from the creature comforts that one might find in the New China World shopping com-plex in Beijing or at the Portman Ritz-Carlton Hotel in Shanghai. They are escorted by drivers and English-speaking guides and taken to the finest restaurants, sleep in luxuriously appointed rooms high in the sky with white-glove service catering to their every desire and need. China seems a confident and prosperous country. That's because the "other China" in this nation of 1.3 billion people—the regions where widespread abject poverty still exists—does not appear anywhere on the typical foreigner's travel itinerary.

To be sure, China's prosperity is not an illusion. With an average annual growth rate of 9.7 percent since the late 1970s, China has surpassed Germany to become the world's third largest economy with a GDP of $3.38 trillion, trailing only Japan ($4.38 trillion) and the United States ($13.8 trillion). More than two hundred million Chinese have been lifted above the World Bank's dollar-a-day poverty line. This is indeed a remarkable achievement. According to the World Bank, China's economic progress represents 90 percent of the entire world's poverty reduction in that period of time.[5] However, there are still three hundred million people in China living on less than a dollar a day.[6] Moreover, despite China's rapid economic growth, the per capita share of the gross domestic product is about $2500 per year for China's 1.3 billion residents. By contrast, the per capita GDP of Germany's 82 million inhabitants is $40,400.[7] Even taking into account the lower costs of many goods and services, approximately half of China, or more than seven hundred million people, still live below what would be considered the poverty line in Western nations.[8]

In addition to its sheer magnitude, the poverty problem is exacerbated by deep regional divides and growing inequality. According to official Chinese government statistics, the per capita GDP of Guangzhou, the capital city of Guangdong Province, is five times greater that the per capita GDP of Qinghai, a province in northwest China.[9] On average, urban incomes are four times that of rural areas. Even in other developing societies, urban GDP is rarely above twice the rural income, so China's income inequality is particularly problematic for the country's social cohesion.

Despite the "other China's" invisibility to the outside world, one does not actually have to travel to remote mountainous regions to find crushing poverty. Interior provinces such as Henan in the north and Guangxi in the south are populated by hundreds of millions of peasants who are barely able to subsist by farming. The hundreds of millions who live in the "other China" are so poor that many of them seldom come into contact with cash, and so they mostly trade through barter. They don't have the mobile phones ubiquitous in coastal cities such as Shanghai. Their houses lack running water, indoor plumbing, and heat in the winter. David Youtz, the Hong Kong–based CEO of the nonprofit Mother's Choice, is one of the few Westerners who have ventured into the "other China." Youtz, who, after graduating from Oberlin College in the early '80s, lived with a Chinese family in a small provincial city, notes that "Western news headlines typically focus on China's economic boom and images of China's wealthy elite, so it's easy to forget that most of China, away from the coastal cities, remains a poor country with all the challenges of a developing nation."[10] BBC reporter Peter Day traveled just two hours southwest of Beijing to the Muslim village of Ningxia. There he found its eighteen thousand inhabitants living in manmade caves.[11] In Henan province in central China, *New York Times* reporter Howard French met Zhou Zhiwen, a fifty-five-year-old woman who told him, "We're deadly poor. We grow just enough food for ourselves to eat, with no surplus grain." Asked how people in her village survived, Ms. Zhou said it was from relatives who had migrated elsewhere for work. "All of our young people are working elsewhere," she said.[12]

The extreme poverty in rural China has led to a massive migration of young workers. Official statistics number migrant workers between seventy and 120 million, but some believe this "floating population" might be twice this number. Young men leave their villages for jobs in China's dangerous mining industry. Others flock to the cities and work on construction jobs or take other low-paid employment shunned by urban residents. Urban residents disparagingly refer to migrant workers as *mang-lin* or "blind flow." These migrant workers have no social safety net. They have no health insurance, no retirement plans, and no housing rights, all of which are tied to their *danwei* or residence unit in China. Because migrant workers are not residents in the places they work, they are not entitled to any of these social benefits. Most are separated from their families. When they are joined by their families, their children are not entitled to enroll in local schools.

While the young men will often look for work in coal mines or urban construction, the young women head for the factories in coastal and southern China. Most of them have never been on a train before. They travel to a place where a relative or fellow villager might show them the ropes. They arrive in a strange, anonymous place, cut off from their families. Tens of millions of them find work in toy factories, clothing factories, shoe factories, and microelectronic assembly plants. If they are fortunate enough to be hired by one of these factories, they live with three or more other young women in a small dormitory room adjacent to the factory. They eat all their meals in the factory canteen. The norm is for these women to work six days a week, and often they are called upon to work overtime each day, well into the evening hours.

Because of the economic desperation in their home villages, these migrant workers willingly seek out such work. These jobs represent an important economic and social opportunity. Even with pay that often is as low as $70 a month, these workers almost universally will send a quarter or more of their paychecks back home to help their families. The emotional bonds of migrant workers to their families remain strong. These bonds are renewed each lunar New Year when the factories empty out and the workers return by bus and train to their villages. A job in the foreign manufacturing sector can dramatically increase a young migrant worker's social standing and autonomy. In a few years, she can save enough money to build a house in her village, and this in turn might enable her to have some choice in a marriage partner. Pun Ngai, a Hong Kong–based labor activist who spent a year as a worker in an electronics factory in southern China, writes poignantly of the life choices made by these mostly female workers:

> Most of the factory women knew quite well before they left their village that they were going to be working in a sweatshop for twelve hours each day, earning about 500 or 600 renminbi [about $70] each month. They all knew the factory boss would not be lenient and treat them as equal human beings. They knew there was a huge gap between industrial life and rural life. They knew their back-breaking labor was a form of selling their bodies. They knew almost everything. But by engaging in this basic struggle to work, there seemed to be a chance that women workers might be able to transgress their individual "fate" (a term they used often in the workplace) of rural family life.[13]

Despite Pun Ngai's account of their economic and social empowerment, the economic desperation from which migrant workers come and the dreams and aspirations that they travel with, when combined with their naïveté and lack of literacy skills, make them vulnerable to abuse, deceit, and exploitation. What these masses of desperate and uneducated workers find in the factories serving the foreign export sector is a business environment that is perfectly suited to exploiting them.[14]

"Digging to the Bottom": Global Demand for Cheap and Flexible Labor

The phrase "race to the bottom" is often used to describe how brand-name companies search the world over to outsource their manufacturing to the cheapest location and how in response developing countries attempt to attract investment capital by competing with each other through ever-lower wages and harsh working conditions. However, the phrase "race to the bottom" doesn't do the perniciousness of the phenomenon justice. As is evident in China, it is not so much a case of developing countries racing to the bottom as it is a matter of brand-name companies "digging to the bottom" through their outsourcing policies.

The general contours of the "race to the bottom" constitute a familiar globalization narrative. Brand-name companies with labor-intensive manufacturing operations embrace the economic virtues of outsourcing. These companies discover the benefits of bypassing expensive union labor by outsourcing to foreign countries. The dismantling of trade laws restricting the free flow of capital and goods accelerates this trend, as does the sunset of protectionist treaties such as the Multi-State Fiber Agreement. Because the switching costs of manufacturing in one place or another are low, these brand-name companies can pick and choose from a whole globe of poor countries with excess labor. As a result of the competition to attract this investment, poor countries are locked into a fierce competition with each other, and key elements of this competition are weak labor laws and weak enforcement of those laws. China is the big winner in this race to the bottom. Although Vietnam and Indonesia give it regional competition and there is some outsourcing of manufacturing in South Asia and Latin America, China has become the factory floor for the world.

What makes the outsourcing process such a threat to workers is all the "digging to the bottom" that brand-name companies do once they get to China. These global companies are mainly concentrated in a few industries such as toys, shoes, apparel, and electronics. With the possible exception of some electronics products that require more long-range planning, these industries are fashion-driven and seasonal. Orders must be completed not only at minimal cost but also within a short time frame. By waiting until the last minute to give an order and by only parceling out manufacturing orders on an as-needed basis, brand-name retailers are able to reduce inventory costs and reduce the risk of being stuck with unwanted inventory. The brands pass along these risks to factory owners in China. The factory owners in turn pass along the burdens and risks to the workers. Not only is there severe downward pressure on wages because of the cost demands of sourcing agents, workers also are forced to work overtime to meet short production schedules.

If Chinese workers are lucky, they will be paid the minimum wage—which, depending on the local laws, is anywhere from $70 to $100 a month—for their work and they also will be paid for any overtime. However, they have very little leverage to prevent greedy and unscrupulous factory operators from taking advantage of them. There are local minimum-wage laws in China and laws that limit the amount of overtime that workers can be required to work. There are even laws that protect worker health and safety. Minimum legal standards do exist, at least in theory. The problem in China is that these laws are not enforced.

A number of factors contribute to the weak enforcement of laws protecting worker rights. Chief among them is the desire of local officials to attract investment to their region, which causes them to turn a blind eye to labor law violations. Also at work are widespread corruption and bribery among officials who are supposed to be enforcing the laws. Underlying these factors are larger issues that are at the root of many of China's problems—the lack of a free press to report on government corruption and labor abuses, and a weak legal system to enforce labor laws. Because of these systemic issues, it is easy for worker rights abuses to go ignored, and it is very difficult for workers to protect their rights through the legal system. In the face of the restrictions on press freedom and an inhospitable legal system, efforts to publicize labor violations and seek redress through the courts are nonetheless, as we shall see, among the tactics at the forefront of the indigenous Chinese labor movement.

The foregoing complex mixture of supply-side and demand-side forces constitutes a potent recipe for labor abuses. On the supply side, vulnerable

Chinese migrant workers enter a labor market that on the demand side is a perfect storm of foreign brand-name companies outsourcing production, uncaring and often unscrupulous factory managers, and a weak regulatory environment that works hand-in-hand with local corruption. These elements work in vicious synergy to enable the systematic and widespread exploitation of workers in China's export sector.

High and Low: CSR and Labor Rights in China

In response to the negative publicity heaped upon them by labor rights activists and NGOs, many multinational corporations have adopted corporate social responsibility (CSR) programs. CSR programs primarily consist of codes of conduct for subcontractors and periodic audits of manufacturing facilities. Another key feature of CSR programs is close cooperation with NGOs such as Social Accountability 8000, the Fair Labor Association, and the Ethical Trading Initiative (ETI).[15] Indeed, it is perhaps more precise to refer to such NGOs as "multi-stakeholder initiatives" because of the participation of corporations in their governance structures. In the decade or so since the CSR movement was born, a veritable social responsibility industrial complex has emerged. In addition to multinational corporations and cooperatively minded NGOs, an army of consultants, for-profit and not-for-profit inspectors, and academics have participated in CSR programs. Hardly a week goes by, it seems, without some CSR conference or symposium. With so many people and financial resources involved in CSR, it is fair to ask whether the effort has been worthwhile. Is CSR helping to end or at least ameliorate the systematic exploitation and abuse of third world factory workers? Or is CSR merely a loincloth to cover the hypocrisy of multinational companies concerned only about brand image? The truth is somewhere between these two extremes. There are indeed significant and systemic problems with CSR that severely affect its credibility and effectiveness. At the same time, despite its ample and evident faults, the resources devoted to CSR make it possible to bring discreet, marginal improvements to workers on a scale not otherwise possible.

The problems and shortcomings of the CSR movement are on full display in China. In assessing the effectiveness of CSR, it is important to understand at the outset that because it is a private and voluntary system, the movement only covers a fraction of export-sector workers. A useful way to understand the limitations of the CSR system is to think of it as a pyramid. At the very bottom of this pyramid are laborers who work in private-sector factories that manufacture for the domestic market. They are far outside the CSR system. Also outside the system are another group of workers in the second tier of the pyramid. It is difficult to estimate the exact numbers, but it seems safe to say that the majority of factory workers in the Chinese export sector work in factories that manufacture for brands that are far less well-known than famous global brands such as Liz Claiborne, Nike, or Disney. As a consequence, these factories are too small and therefore extremely unlikely to engender muckraking investigations by NGOs or the press. They operate under the radar of the Chinese government and the antisweatshop movement. Tens of thousands of such factories, which might have two hundred to a couple of thousand workers each, dot the landscape in the manufacturing hubs of Guangdong, Fujian, Zhejiang, and Jiangsu provinces. Most of them have never been visited by a labor rights monitor.

The third tier of the pyramid consists of companies that have insincere and hypocritical CSR programs. The effectiveness of factory monitoring is crucially dependent on the seriousness with which brand-name companies approach it. There is considerable variation in the integrity with which companies undertake CSR initiatives. For too many companies, "ethical sourcing" is an empty public relations gesture without any real meaning. "For the half-assed company, there are also half-assed monitoring firms," writes former labor monitor T. A. Frank. "These specialize in performing as many brief, understaffed inspections as they can fit in a day. That gives their clients plausible deniability: problems undiscovered are problems avoided, and any later trouble can be blamed on the compliance monitors. It is a cozy understanding between client, monitoring company, and supplier that manages to benefit everyone but the workers."[16]

The brand-name companies that practice half-hearted "CSR light" are the easiest prey for campaigns and exposés by NGOs, labor activists, and the press. On the eve of the opening of the Hong Kong Disneyland, Students and Scholars Against Corporate Misbehavior (SACOM), a Hong Kong–based NGO, launched a "Looking for Mickey Mouse's Conscience" campaign. SACOM secretly investigated and then publicized the miserable labor conditions at eleven factories manufacturing for Disney in the Pearl River Delta region of southern China. Among the problems uncovered were nonpayment of wages, excessive and forced overtime, withholding of social security, safety and environmental problems, and substandard living conditions in the worker dormitories. "There is no fairytale ending for overworked Disney toy workers," commented SACOM'S chief co-ordinator Jenny Chan.[17] In December 2007, the New York–based National Labor Committee issued a report, *A Wal-Mart Christmas: Brought to You by a Sweatshop in China*. The report profiled the Wal-Mart subcontractor Guangzhou Huanya, a factory of eight thousand workers that manufactures Christmas ornaments for Wal-Mart and other companies. According to the report, "Every single labor law in China, along with internationally recognized worker rights standards, are being systematically violated on a daily basis."[18]

The companies in this third tier face a basic choice. When confronted with the evidence of their inadequate monitoring, they can—like Wal-Mart and Disney—tough out the resulting bad publicity and continue with a half-hearted CSR program. Alternatively, they can attempt to move up to the fourth tier or the top of the pyramid of CSR. At the top of the CSR pyramid are companies such as Mattel, Nike, adidas, and the Gap. These companies, which have been stung by the glare of bad publicity, devote substantial financial and human resources to CSR. They have adopted all of the hallmarks of effective CSR programs. They have agreed to independent monitoring of their plants. Their monitoring criteria are detailed and specific. Mattel, for example, has a seventy-five-page checklist for inspections. They have agreed to unannounced inspections. They have also agreed to post the results of their audits publicly, usually on the company website.[19]

The leading-edge companies at the top of the pyramid not only monitor their subcontractors but also try to devise strategies for remedying the underlying problems uncovered by the factory audit.[20] Hong Kong–based William Anderson, the head of adidas's Department of Social and Environmental Affairs for Asia Pacific, supervises a staff of forty, including specialists in employment law, health and safety, and even social scientists. Companies such as adidas have learned that monitoring alone accomplishes very little.[21] The real challenge is to do something about the causes behind the audit failures. Anderson says that "fixing the underlying problems is a lot more complicated than just monitoring."

The most disappointing aspect of CSR is that even well-intentioned "top of the pyramid" companies that hire reputable monitoring firms are easily and frequently deceived by faulty audits. The theory behind monitoring is that if factories are found to be out of compliance with local labor laws regarding such things as minimum wages, overtime, and child labor, the brand-name companies whose goods are being manufactured can either pressure the supplier into compliance or sever their ties completely and find an alternative supplier. However, many factory owners in China have responded to the social responsibility industrial complex by creating a kind of parallel universe of social responsibility evasion and deception. Just as CSR conferences in the United States, Europe, and Hong Kong are held to promote CSR, newspapers in southern China routinely contain advertisements about "classes" that teach factory owners how to deceive auditors. One article in *Southern Weekend,* a major newspaper in the Pearl River Delta manufacturing hub, describes CSR as a "cat and mouse game." It describes a two-day class costing approximately $300 that teaches managers "how to elude SA8000 and European and U.S. buyers' inspections and get SA8000 certification."[22] Sadly, these evasion efforts have paid off. Former labor monitor T. A. Frank reports that "the major challenge of inspections was simply staying ahead of the factories we monitored. False time cards and payroll records, whole days spent coaching employees on how to lie during interviews, and even renaming certain factory buildings in order to create a smaller Potemkin village—all of these were techniques used by contractors to try to fool us." Frank offers no illusions about the auditing process: "Unfortunately, we missed stuff. All inspections do. And sometimes it was embarrassing."[23]

So how do we evaluate the impact of CSR on China's sweatshop problem? As we have seen, there are significant and systemic problems with CSR that severely limit its effectiveness. The CSR system does not reach most Chinese workers. When it does reach workers in the export sector, it often does so in a half-hearted and hypocritical manner. And even when CSR is practiced with integrity, factory audits are often evaded by unscrupulous subcontractors. Beyond these operational difficulties, CSR has deeper systemic problems. What has failed to emerge in over a decade of factory monitoring is any positive marketplace premium for ethical behavior.

The market continues to punish companies that suffer negative publicity when confrontational NGOs, such as the National Labor Committee or the Workers Rights Consortium, expose conditions at their subcontractors. However, after a decade of meetings, symposiums, and workshops, the social responsibility industrial complex has failed to develop any market-place value in their various certification procedures. There are a number of reasons behind this failure. First and foremost is the lack of credibility of the CSR system as a whole because of the many examples of hypocrisy and ineptitude in monitoring that continue to be exposed by confrontational NGOs and the media. A second reason is the continued balkanization of CSR. NGOs such as the Fair Labor Association, SA8000, and ETI continue to go their separate ways, each with their own standards. And while these multi-stakeholder groups have worked closely with industry and been financially supported by it for over a decade, they have failed to invest sufficient energy or thought in creating value for their certification systems. As a result, consumers who might be willing to pay more for ethically manufactured products have no way to pay a "sweat-free" premium to express positive support for antisweatshop efforts. Stung by a story in the *Observer* that documented child labor in its Asia suppliers, Gap Inc. reportedly is considering adopting a "sweat-free" label for its clothing.[24] But after a decade of CSR hypocrisy and failed implementation, who is really going to believe in the integrity of a "sweat-free" label any more?

Because of CSR's many and manifest shortcomings and limitations, it is tempting to dismiss CSR in China as a complete failure. This, however, would be unfair. It is better to think of it as a flawed but noble experiment that has yielded significant benefits for some Chinese workers. Despite its faults, the resources devoted to CSR make it possible to bring marginal improvements in working conditions on a scale not otherwise possible. Based on conversations with company executives, it is fair to say that the factories that manufacture for the ten to twenty companies at the top of the CSR pyramid employ anywhere between one to two million workers. Thus, although CSR cannot possibly "solve" the sweatshop problem, it can make a meaningful difference in the lives of many workers. One auditor working with Mattel made the case for CSR as follows: "We've made their lives a lot easier. Especially the young women. At one plant we visited, it used to be that if you lived on the sixth floor of their dorm, if you wanted water you had to walk down to the ground level, pick up a bucket, and you dragged this heavy bucket up six flights, and that's how you washed yourself. Now we got them water on the sixth floor."[25] Labor rights, of course, are not just about the ability to have running water. Labor rights are also about forced overtime, minimum wages, child labor, and other big issues. At the end of the day, however, the CSR movement must be measured by how much it improves the lives of ordinary workers in China. By this measure, while CSR is a limited and highly flawed system, it has been able to achieve some marginal improvements for workers on a significant scale.

From the Boardroom to the Barricades: NGOs in China

Despite the efforts of brand-name companies to manage the labor issues in their supply chain, many in the NGO community insist that the CSR system as a whole has been too imperfectly administered and inadequate in scope to make a significant dent in China's overall sweatshop problem. As a consequence, activists continue to "name and shame" global brands by exposing the more egregious labor practices of their subcontractors. They maintain that true progress on labor rights can occur only if Chinese workers are allowed to organize into independent trade unions that give voice to their interests and rights. Whereas the tool of choice for CSR is the clipboard, these activists prefer the megaphone. They believe progress will come when independent union leaders can amplify worker concerns and engage in collective bargaining. Indeed, a vast ideological gulf has opened up between some in the NGO community who continue to cooperate with the CSR movement and others that have begun to question the fundamental premises of CSR.

Throughout the past decade there has been considerable ambivalence among NGOs about cooperating with CSR efforts. Over time, a "bad cop, good cop" pattern has emerged. Some NGOs, the "bad cops," remained highly critical of CSR and continued to "name and shame" companies by conducting exposés and public campaigns. This caused companies to run into the arms of the "good cops," NGOs and multi-stakeholder groups that offered independent monitoring services. Although the two kinds of NGOs followed divergent strategies, the "good cop, bad cop" phenomenon made their activities synergistic.[26] However, when one discusses CSR with workers in Hong Kong and with China-based NGOs it is clear that they have reached a new and significant ideological divide both with CSR and with the NGOs that cooperate with companies.

Apo Leung of the Hong Kong–based Asia Monitor Resource Center typifies the growing disenchantment with the CSR approach to China's sweatshop problem. Leung, a former reporter who started doing grass-roots labor organizing over two decades ago, has little patience for the public relations patois of CSR. "Through CSR, labour rights are in danger of being privatized and integrated even more deeply into market logic as an economic factor," writes Leung. "Another danger is that the promising momentum of new radical ideas and direct action will be lost in the global north and be completely co-opted by the proliferation of CSR initiatives. CSR may contain the elements of a social movement, but increasingly it is a movement determined by capital rather than by labor."[27]

Leung's disillusionment stems in part from an unsatisfactory experi-ence that he and his colleagues at the Hong Kong Confederation of Trade Unions had in attempting to cooperate with the Ethical Trading Initia-tive. United Kingdom–based ETI is multi-stakeholder initiative, includ-ing companies, NGOs, and unions. Although Leung is not critical of the ETI colleagues with whom he has worked, he and others in the Chinese labor movement became disenchanted with the overall philosophical ap-proach of ETI and its CSR partners. In particular, Leung questioned the notion that every project needs to be promoted as a "win-win" to become viable and worth pursuing: "If a project aims to increase worker participation, then this must be made clear to all involved and the persua-sive argument of increased productivity and brand recognition should not be induced to get corporations on board who ultimately do not wish to see more than a successful 'China project' to show their clients and shareholders."[28]

What is the alternative? If labor activists reject the fundamental premises of CSR, what do they propose in its place? Groups such as the Chinese Working Women Network (CWWN), led by Pun Ngai, and Students and Scholars Against Corporate Misbehavior (SACOM), headed by Jenny Chan, offer one answer—worker empowerment. Working at the grassroots level, these NGOs would rather empower workers to pro-tect themselves than rely on the fickle and unreliable noblesse oblige of the CSR movement. To be sure, these organizations are small and underfunded but their vision for labor rights is a big one. The problem, of course, is that if the organizing efforts of CWWN and SACOM ever do achieve a critical mass they will run smack up against a monumental roadblock. All labor activities come under the aegis of the ACFTU, an arm of the Chinese government. Before we consider the role that the ACFTU is attempting to play, it is worth considering developments in Chinese labor law.

China's New Labor Contract Law

As NGOs continue to pressure global brand-name companies and these companies respond by developing CSR programs, the Chinese government belatedly has attempted to become relevant in protecting the rights and interests of migrant workers. Low-wage manufacturing jobs in the export sector represent important opportunities for migrant workers from interior provinces to improve their lot. However, the rising inequality between urban and rural areas and between the coastal and interior provinces, along with persistent labor issues in the export sector, has become a source of increasing civil unrest, threatening China's social and political stability. The government is thus under increasing pressure to do something to improve the lives of migrant workers.

Another impetus for reform was a June 2007 incident that was little noticed outside of China but which upset and shamed many within the country. Hundreds of parents whose children had been abducted in Henan Province were shocked to learn that their children had been sold to work in brick factories in Henan and Shanxi provinces. As many as a thousand children were abducted. Television reports showed workers sleeping on bricks with doors wired to prevent their escape. "We wanted to run but we couldn't," said one child worker. "I tried once and was beaten." Even the *People's Daily*, the official mouthpiece of the Communist Party, conceded that tacit approval or even collusion from poorly funded local governments was to blame. "At present, some grassroots governments are grappling with huge debts, so they are sluggish in administration and even gain incomes illegally, causing instability in rural areas."[29]

In the context of the current global financial crisis, worker interests are under increasing stress. Even before the crisis, enforcing labor standards risked driving foreign investment to neighboring low-wage countries such as Vietnam, Thailand, Indonesia, Bangladesh, and India, or to other parts of the world, such as Latin America. By early 2009, global demand for Chinese manufactured goods had contracted dramatically. As a consequence, approximately 35 million Chinese workers (representing about 8 percent of the non-agricultural labor force) lost their jobs. The government has responded to these new economic realities by formally introducing legal worker protection initiatives while recognizing that it will be some years before those initiatives are fully implemented.

The most important pro-worker initiative is the new Labor Contract Law that went into effect in January 2008. The first draft of the proposed regulations to implement that law was issued in May of the same year. The new law is an important watershed in China's transition from a centrally planned economy and socialist society to a free market where procedural legal rights replace substantive socialist entitlements. As the "iron rice bowl" is dismantled, China faces an array of challenges in providing citizens with a safety net in social benefits such as housing, medical benefits, retirement income, and education. In most of these areas, it is still unclear what institutions and norms will emerge to fill the social security void. In the labor relations context, however, the contours of this institutional and ideological transformation are becoming clear. The government is transitioning from the role of employer and guarantor to that of rule maker and regulator of private contracts and transactions in the free market.

The new Labor Contract Law marks a transition from a labor system in which the government was the sole employer and where a worker's life could be so crucially affected by the arbitrary whims of an immediate supervisor, to one in which employees—for the moment only in theory—enjoy substantive and procedural workplace rights. Certainly, workers have fewer social welfare guarantees than within the "iron rice bowl." However, many worker interests will be recognized as substantive legal rights and guarded by procedural rights. That the Labor Contract Law was promulgated after substantial input from workers further serves to underscore its significance in advancing worker rights to procedural justice.

The new law, passed in June 2007, requires that employers provide written contracts to all long-term workers, and that short-term workers be hired as long-term workers with social insurance benefits after their contracts have been renewed twice. It also contains severance pay provisions and tightens the conditions that allow a company to fire a worker. The law empowers company-based branches of the state-run All China Federation of Trade Unions to bargain with employers over salaries, bonuses, training, and other benefits and job duties. A previously circulated draft of the law had required ACFTU permission to lay off workers, but this was changed in the final version to require prior consultation only.

These worker-protection provisions were the result of Western-style lobbying. "When the Labor Contract Law was being drafted," notes one Chinese lawyer, "the business community was unhappy with the provisions eliminating the ability to fire an employee at will and it made its views known to the government."[30] A few months after the first draft was circulated in 2004, Chinese leaders took the unprecedented step of seeking public comment. The response was extraordinary. The government reported 191,849 comments. Some came from large companies such as General Electric and Microsoft and umbrella trade organizations such as the American Chamber of Commerce. However, the overwhelming majority came from ordinary workers organized by the ACFTU's campaign to pass the new law.

Because of the global economic slowdown and the underdeveloped nature of legal rights and the legal system in China, it will take many years before the Labor Contract Law achieves its "on paper" potential. If the law were to be enforced vigorously, it would have significant economic effects on the manufacturing industry. The requirement that all employees be given written contracts will impose administrative costs on firms. In addition, firms will have less flexibility to hire and fire. The severance clauses will increase operational costs as will the requirement that worker benefits be paid. There are already in place minimum wage laws, but written contracts will make it more likely that the minimum wage will actually be paid. Another unknown factor that could increase costs further would be if the ACFTU actually starts behaving like a real union and, as contemplated by the law, presses for collective bargaining gains for workers at the factory, regional, or industry level.

How much higher will labor costs be as a result of the new law? Estimates among an informal poll of factory operators vary from 5 percent to 40 percent. The most common estimate that one hears among factory operators is that costs will increase 30 percent. The actual costs will depend primarily on two factors: (1) the degree of compliance with legal requirements prior to the passage of the law (the higher prepassage compliance is, the lower the postpassage costs will be) and (2) the ability of firms to efficiently absorb the administrative costs of compliance. The result of both of these factors is that in the long term the foreign export manufacturing sector will experience significant consolidation. Firms such as Yue Yuen Holdings, the largest manufacturer of athletic shoes, and electronics manufacturing giant Hon Hai Precision Industry, each employing hundreds of thousands of workers, will enjoy an increased competitive advantage over small firms that employ only a few hundred workers each. The larger firms are those already likely to be in compliance with minimum wage laws because of the scrutiny of NGOs and the need to attract workers. The larger firms also can more easily absorb, because of their scale and their existing administrative overhead, the costs of compliance with the contracting provisions. They can, moreover, establish longer term relations with big brand names to minimize the costs imposed by the law's restrictions on, and penalties for, firing workers. When all of these factors are taken into account, the new law, if and when it is enforced, is likely to cause many smaller firms to go out of business and others to merge to achieve the economies of scale necessary to absorb the higher costs of compliance.

Although industry consolidation can buffer some of the loss of comparative advantage for the Chinese manufacturing industry, in passing the new labor law China has slowed the pace of its "race to the bottom." It is risking that brand names will look elsewhere for their manufacturing needs to countries with lower wages and weaker labor laws. Vietnam is often mentioned as such a destination. Even before the passage of the Labor Contract Law, Vietnamese labor costs were, by the estimate of the Chinese government, one third that of China. Inevitably, some firms will be attracted to Vietnam and other lower costs countries. China must hope that the productivity of its workforce and the relative efficiency of its entire supply chain will outweigh increased labor costs associated with the new law.

In the short term, the new law has had a wide range of effects, some in ways that the law intended but in other ways perverse. Even before the law went into effect, some large manufacturing firms were engaging in attempts at evasion. Perhaps the most egregious example was Huawei Technologies in the southern province of Guangdong, which called on workers who had been with the company for more than eight years to "voluntarily" resign. Huawei, which employed more than seven thousand workers, intended to rehire some and sign them to a contract and to pay compensation to the workers they chose not to rehire. The scheme was designed to avoid the provision in the new law that required employees who had worked with the company for more than ten years to be given "permanent" status. Huawei was hoping the resignations would start the clock ticking all over again. Huawei's plan was widely condemned in the worker community and eventually the ACFTU persuaded the company to back away from its plans.[31]

Smaller firms have continued to follow a "disappearing" strategy, moving further inland to evade government enforcement of labor laws. Mr. Chen and Mr. Wu are typical small-factory owners.[32] Mr. Chen, the Taiwanese owner-operator of a two-hundred-person toy factory in Guangzhou, was aware that there was a new labor contract law and had even attended a government seminar on compliance with the law. When prompted he proudly produced the booklet handed out at the seminar, but it was clear that he had not read it and was unfamiliar with any of the provisions of the law. Mr. Wu was only vaguely aware of the new law and he had not made the slightest effort to become familiar with it. What is behind this lackadaisical attitude? In many ways the responses of Mr. Chen and Mr. Wu to the new law are perfectly rational. They are operating in an environment in which laws are rarely enforced and easily evaded, perhaps with a small bribe now and then to be on the safe side. In this context the new labor contract law is more of the same—another empty law that can be flouted. It will take some time before the workers in small plants reap the benefits of the new law and Chen and Wu are betting that they are too small fish to be of much interest to local authorities.

These reactions by company owners—ranging from head-in-the-sand avoidance to outright attempts to circumvent the law—reflect the complexity and diversity of the factories producing for the export sector as well as the current state of the Chinese political and legal system. Yet unknown is how stringently the new law will be enforced, against what kinds of firms, and in what locations.

The Role of the ACFTU in the Antisweatshop Movement

Traditionally, Chinese workers have not viewed the ACFTU as a "real" union such as one might find in other parts of the world. In fact, in a 1988 survey the union conducted about itself, less than 10 percent of members believed that the union did a good job of representing them and 25 percent agreed that the union "only collected dues and conducted recreational activities."[33] The traditional role of the ACFTU was to provide services to workers such as hobby centers and sports outings. It did not attempt to represent workers against management or bargain collectively over layoffs, working conditions, and pay. The ACFTU has always been an arm of the state and controlled by the Communist Party. Many of its top officials are also top officials in the Communist Party.

The ACFTU calls itself a union "with Chinese characteristics," concerned more with harmonious relations than with confrontation. In 1989, when workers took to the streets to show support for the students occupying Tiananmen Square, the ACFTU sided with the government. It is jarring to hear a labor union official state the order of his priorities as "stability" followed by "worker rights," but this is just how the vice chairman of the Hubei Province chapter of the ACFTU described the mission of his union to a group of U.S. union officials in November 2007.[34]

Like just about every other institution in the reform era, however, the ACFTU is changing. According to the Hong Kong–based NGO *China Labor Bulletin,* the union lost over thirty million members due to layoffs in connection with the restructuring of state-owned enterprises. To remain relevant, the ACFTU's focus thus turned to workers in the newly emerging private sector. Because every company it organizes must pay 2 percent of its payroll to the union, the ACFTU has a financial incentive to step up its organizing activities. One group targeted by the union has been migrant workers. Before 2001, migrant workers were not even eligible for union representation. In recent years, however, the ACFTU has made a concerted effort to organize migrant workers, especially those who work for foreign companies. At the end of 2006, the ACFTU claimed to have almost forty-one million migrant workers as members (though some dispute this figure). The most high profile example of this shift in strategy was the ACFTU's successful campaign to do something no U.S. union has hitherto been able to accomplish—unionize Wal-Mart.

The ACFTU's campaign against Wal-Mart began in 2003. Initially, Wal-Mart—as it does elsewhere in the world—resisted unionization. The company claimed that no workers had expressed interest in forming a union and thus it would not allow ACFTU representatives into any of its stores. For three years Wal-Mart and the ACFTU engaged in a standoff that even caught the attention of President Hu Jintao who exhorted the ACFTU to "do a better job of building [Communist] Party organizations and trade unions in foreign-invested enterprises."[35] The logjam was broken in 2006 when Ke Yunlong, a college-educated worker employed in the frozen meats section, organized a group of employees in the southeastern city of Quanzhou. Working with the ACFTU, Ke conducted secret meetings offsite and eventually persuaded thirty workers to form a union. In rapid succession, unions were formed in Shenzhen and Nanjing. Eventually, all sixty-two Wal-Mart stores in China were unionized. Wal-Mart joined a growing list of foreign companies with ACFTU unions, including Carrefour, Samsung, McDonald's, Dell, and Kodak. By 2007, the ACFTU claimed to have formed branches at 60 percent of all foreign-owned enterprises, with plans to increase that amount to 80 percent by the end of 2008.

Despite the ACFTU's seeming success with unionizing Wal-Mart, indigenous, independent labor organizers in the region still view it as an arm of a repressive regime. The highly respected labor activist Han Dongfang, who spent two years in jail for his union organizing activities, calls the Wal-Mart ACFTU union an "instant noodle union that gives people false hope."[36] These critics point to the fact that the Wal-Mart ACFTU unions, for all the attention given to them by the Western media, have failed to produce any tangible gains for workers. Apart from one occasion involving a store in Nanchang in Jiangxi Province, where the union persuaded management to reverse a few minor directives, the union has not represented workers in collective bargaining with any of the Wal-Mart stores. To date the Wal-Mart ACFTU unions have been content to provide entertainment and recreational services for members.

As in so many other aspects of Chinese politics, regionalism plays an important factor in determining the independence and effectiveness of the ACFTU in representing workers. Unfortunately, recent studies, one by Xiaodan Zhang and another by Mingwei Liu, suggest that ACFTU unions remain weak where they are needed most—in cities such as Guangzhou where local officials are keen to attract foreign capital and in cities such as Lu'an and Dalian where state-owned enterprises are laying off workers.[37] Local ACFTU units in export-oriented areas are not in any position to upset the apple cart when it comes to attracting foreign investment. So they are very likely in these areas to side with management against migrant workers. Moreover, it is precisely in areas where workers have significant material differences with employers and where there is a possibility of confrontation and conflict that the ACFTU reverts to its traditional role in promoting a "harmonious society."

The ACFTU's mixed success in unionizing Wal-Mart has caused considerable hand-wringing in the international labor movement as it scrambles to devise a "China strategy." Berkeley-based labor scholar Katie Quan has remarked that "the debate among international labor leaders has shifted from *whether* to engage with Chinese workers to *how*." The question of how to engage with China has become a matter of some disagreement among labor leaders in the West. Some union leaders, like Andy Stern of the Service Employees International Union (SEIU), sound like starry-eyed CEOs seduced by the China "market." These officials have seized on the fact that China represents an organizing challenge of an unprecedented scale and that the ACFTU, which claimed at the end of 2006 to have over 210 million members, still represents the best chance to create positive change in China. They speak wistfully of the "enormity" of China and, like their CEO counterparts, they've decided to team with the best joint-venture partner they can find—one with good connections to the government, no less, the ACFTU. SEIU officials worked closely with the ACFTU and offered tactical help in unionizing Wal-Mart. Despite the fact that the actual accomplishments by the Wal-Mart ACFTU union have been meager at best, the Western media has portrayed the SEIU's participation in the formation of the Wal-Mart union as a significant "win" for the "Change to Win" labor coalition of which SEIU is the prime mover. What exactly SEIU has won in China or for whom is not exactly clear, however.

What is at stake in the decisions of international labor leaders about how to engage with Chinese workers? What could possibly be wrong with working with the ACFTU, which has massive scale and potential power to improve the lives of workers? The danger of engaging too closely with the ACFTU is that it could undermine the activities of a small but important independent labor movement in China. An editorial by Apo Leung's *Asian Labor Update* cautioned international labor leaders from getting too cozy with the ACFTU at the expense of independent grassroots organizers: "Seeing the ACFTU as a partner or a legitimate counterpart...is potentially fraught with difficulties—such contacts can be used as propaganda by the ACFTU and may also disappoint workers inside China who seek to see western unions take a stand in supporting their struggles and not siding with the ACFTU. Union efforts should be put into supporting workers in need, instead of befriending a union which is part of the power structure in China."[38]

Even as the ACFTU expands its membership base, independent, grassroots labor rights advocacy is also growing. Indeed, one of the most exciting aspects of the new Labor Contract Law is that it has galvanized workers' interest in their legal rights. Diana Beaumont of the *China Labor Bulletin* reports that "throughout southern China news of the law's provisions is rapidly spreading among ordinary workers. They are becoming increasingly aware of their legal rights. What we are also seeing is a growing group of self-trained worker advocates attempting to use the new law to achieve worker gains through the legal system."[39] This movement is often spearheaded by brave migrant workers who began by pressing their own individual claims and have grown to take on leadership roles. "Lily," for example, is in her late twenties and lives with her husband and baby girl in Shenzhen. She works out of a secret office organizing workers at local factories.[40] There are hundreds of untrained lawyers such as Qi Yunhui, a native of Hubei Province in central China who first migrated to Shenzhen in 2002 to work in a shoe factory. For the past five years he has been representing migrant clients who work in factories manufacturing toys, electronics, shoes, apparel, and other export goods. To be sure, these self-trained worker-advocates face enormous obstacles in their efforts to secure justice. Apart from the broad institutional problems in China's legal system described in chapter 5, it is very difficult for migrant workers to prevail in legal actions against companies and government officials who often exercise unfair and corrupt influence over judges. Representing migrant workers against businesses can also be dangerous work. Late in 2007, two men wielding knives attacked Huang Qingnan of the Dagongzhe Migrant Worker Center in Shenzhen, leaving him in the hospital for weeks.[41]

Mindful of the struggles of grassroots labor organizers in China, some unions, such as the Teamsters and the AFL-CIO, are proceeding more cautiously in China, not sure exactly how to engage with Chinese workers in a country that does not honor the right to form independent trade unions and to freely express political opinions. Leaders such as Tim Beaty of the Teamsters are circumspect in engaging with the ACFTU. Although Beaty has made several trips to China to meet with his organizing counterparts, he worries that by engaging with the ACFTU they will be helping the government to "co-opt" the labor movement.[42]

Returning from a trip to China in December 2007, AFL-CIO general counsel Jon Hiatt was decidedly sober in his assessment of the ACFTU: "While the ACFTU is constitutionally bound to protect workers' rights, it is simultaneously required to promote productivity and enforce workplace discipline. And as an official arm of the government and the Communist Party, the ACFTU in recent times has typically focused on the latter at the expense of the former." In his trip to China, Hiatt met with migrant workers who were working as legal advocates, NGO leaders who themselves were injured in China's export sector who were now advocating for other victims of industrial accidents, and organizers who work with migrant workers creating factory and dormitory networks. Hiatt was equally sober in assessing these grassroots efforts: "These courageous and dedicated organizations and their leadership all seemed to recognize that their models were not long-term or broad-based solutions to the protection of worker rights in China. Rather, they understood that what they are offering has relatively marginal impact, and can have no lasting effect unless they serve to put pressure on the government to accept an independent trade union movement."[43]

The Future of the Antisweatshop Movement in China

In the coming decade, the antisweatshop movement in China will undergo extraordinary structural changes. The private-sector CSR solution has proven to be a highly flawed stopgap measure. Although the CSR movement played a modestly useful role in protecting worker rights in the past decade, CSR will likely play a diminished role in protecting worker rights in the future. In place of CSR, the coming decade will witness the rise of trade unionism as the primary response to the labor rights of migrant workers. The biggest unknown in the next decade will be how independent such trade unions will be. Will the ACFTU evolve into a true independent union that represents workers or will it continue to function as an arm of the Communist Party? Obviously the answer to that question depends in part on whether the legal and political system in China will in general progress to a point where democracy and human rights will flourish to a much greater extent than they do now. Also unclear is how the global financial crisis will affect the pace and trajectory of labor reforms. As overall global demand for Chinese products slows, and as China rebalances from an export-oriented economy to one that is more focused on internal markets, there will be enormous temptation to maintain profitability by squeezing workers.

The question facing international labor leaders in the next decade is how to responsibly engage with Chinese workers. The danger for union leaders that engage too uncritically is that they unwittingly could be used to legitimize China's labor rights record. They must be careful not to enter into the same kind of complacent partnership with the ACFTU that Western business leaders have settled into with the party-state. Moreover, as we have seen, independent grassroots organizers and advocates are playing an important role in advancing worker rights, and they deserve the material and moral support of the international labor movement.

Because there really is no way to predict with certainty how the ACFTU will evolve, the most responsible approach to engagement is a cautious one, such as that proposed by the International Trade Union Confederation (ITUC) late in 2007. Reversing its earlier decision to refuse contacts with the ACFTU, the ITUC "rules of engagement" emphasize substantive issues, focusing on training sessions and sharing of expertise on questions of health and safety and collective bargaining. Crucially, however, they reserve the right and announce the intention to continue to speak out critically on China's worker and human rights obligations. Even this policy of cautious engagement was opposed by some of the ITUC's members—including the Polish union Solidarnosc (Solidarity), the Dutch Trade Union Federation (Federatie Nederlandse Vakbeweging or FNV), and Hong Kong trade unions, all of whom are concerned that support for the ACFTU will undermine the fledgling grassroots labor organizations.[44] Nevertheless, it strikes a judicious balance between unnecessarily isolating China and engaging with it in a responsible way that can help China evolve on a path to democracy and human rights. This kind of cautiousness is wholly appropriate for labor unions—which are, after all, organizationally and ideologically committed to advocating for the rights of workers. Engagement with the ACFTU makes sense only if that association will help push the ACFTU toward a stronger worker orientation and ultimately greater independence from the government and Communist Party.

The idea of "cautious and critical engagement" might also serve as a relevant model for how all foreigners should responsibly operate in China. It is not an adequate moral standard simply to be an uncritical participant in China's rapidly growing economy. *How* foreigners engage with China will help to determine whether and how quickly China progresses toward democracy and human rights in the decade to come.

3

DRUG SAFETY RACES TO THE BOTTOM

The Need for "Safe Trade" in Drugs and Other Products Manufactured in China

Just after the New Year in 2008, two children undergoing dialysis at St. Louis Children's Hospital experienced severe allergic reactions. Their eyelids swelled, their heartbeats quickened, and their blood pressure dropped within two minutes of being hooked up to dialysis machines for their regular treatments. The attending physicians at the hospital had seen similar reactions a few weeks earlier. At the time, the doctors assumed it was a problem with the sterilization of the dialysis equipment. When the second incidents occurred, Dr. Alexis M. Edward realized that "we really need to report this."[1]

After learning about Dr. Edward's findings, the federal Centers for Disease Control and Prevention (CDC) posted Internet notices and advisories about the unusual adverse events. Within two days, the CDC received reports of similar reactions among fifty adult dialysis patients in six states. The cause of the allergic reactions turned out to be contamination in the blood thinner heparin, which was used in dialysis as well as in treating heart attack victims and in heart surgery. By November 2008 the CDC counted over seven hundred reports of serious side effects among heparin users and perhaps as many as eighty-one deaths attributable to contaminated heparin. Baxter International recalled heparin products in the United States as did companies in Canada, Japan, Italy, Denmark, France, and Germany after eighty German patients fell ill from allergic reactions to heparin.[2]

Eventually, the supply chain led back to a contaminated ingredient manufactured in China. Baxter bought the adulterated heparin—derived from pig intestines—from Scientific Protein Laboratories, co-owned by a Bethesda, Maryland-based leveraged buyout firm called American Strategies and a Chinese company, Changzhou SPL. It turned out that the Changzhou SPL plant had never been inspected by either U.S. or Chinese authorities. The supply chain for the adulterated product stretched even more remotely from the grasp of either Chinese or U.S. government regulators. Changzhou SPL purchased the adulterated heparin from two wholesalers who in turn purchased it from smaller producers, many of whom oversee crude family-run operations that extract raw heparin from pig intestines.

When the FDA finally got around to investigating the plant in February 2008, it found that the active ingredients from Changzhou SPL were adulterated with a cheap, unapproved ingredient—oversulphated chondroitin sulphate (OSCS), modified to mimic heparin. OSCS is not ordinarily found in nature. It is created through the chemical synthesis of chondroitin sulphate, which is derived from animal cartilage and used as a nutritional supplement. Scientific Protein Laboratories claimed that the contaminant was already in the crude heparin by the time it found its way to Changzhou SPL. Because OSCS mimics heparin, it was not detected by routine quality control testing. The FDA found that anywhere from 2 percent to 50 percent of the suspect heparin samples consisted of OSCS. The introduction of a cheap, chemically synthesized contaminant designed to mimic heparin and evade detection suggested the disturbing probability that the contamination was deliberate rather than accidental.

Thanks to the vigilance of the doctors at St. Louis Children's Hospital and the quick response of the CDC, the potential harm of the heparin contamination was limited to eighty-one deaths. However, the heparin incident could have been far more tragic if the U.S. public health safety alert system had not caught the problem. The tainted heparin joined an alarming list of adulterated and misbranded drugs manufactured in China that have resulted in hundreds of deaths and an untold number of injuries, presenting a major threat to public health and safety worldwide.

In this chapter, I examine the root causes of China's systemic and pervasive product safety problems, in particular emphasizing the inadequacy of regulatory oversight by the Chinese government and Western regulators. I then go on to describe the policies and procedures Western pharmaceutical companies need to put in place if they want to continue to source raw materials and active pharmaceutical ingredients in an ethical and responsible manner.

The Global Consequences of China's Product Safety Problems

Until the heparin incident, the most serious safety problems of Chinese exports occurred in third world countries. This resulted in a false sense of security in the United States and Europe. A very few investigative reporters attempted to call attention to the global threat posed by China's safety problems, including Walt Bogdanich and Jake Hooker of the *New York Times* (who were awarded a Pulitzer Prize for their efforts). For the most part, however, complacency and ignorance reigned even when other countries suffered tragedy.

In Haiti, a Chinese chemical company sold a toxic ingredient that made its way into cough syrup that killed more than a hundred children.[3] In Panama, tainted cough medicine killed more than one hundred people. Instead of glycerin, a nonactive fluid used to mix many drug formulations, the cough medicine had been made with diethylene glycol, a cheap, industrial grade and toxic syrup more commonly used in antifreeze.[4] The motive for substituting ingredients was simple greed. Diethylene glycol costs less than half that of glycerin. In South Asia, investigators traced a flood of fake antimalarial drugs, containing starch, to an illegal factory in China's Guangdong Province. The counterfeit medication threatened to undermine global public health efforts to fight a disease that kills more than a million people each year.[5]

Chinese citizens suffer the worst consequences of the country's manufacturing safety problems. In 2008, contaminated milk and infant formula sickened more than 300,000 children, six of whom died. Chinese producers watered down and then added the industrial chemical melamine to increase nitrogen content and to give the appearance of normal protein levels in test-ing. Over a dozen countries around the world have discovered melamine in products such as chocolate, yogurt, frozen desserts, biscuits, cake, and cookies. In November 2008, the FDA restricted the entry of all food prod-ucts from China that contained milk.[6]

Every year in China thousands of people die or fall ill, many suffering permanent disabilities such as brain damage, from tainted pharmaceuticals. In January 2008, Shanghai police began investigating a Shanghai company that manufactured leukemia drugs, contaminated with vincristine sulfate, that had paralyzed two hundred Chinese patients. Officials at Hualian, a division of the Chinese drug giant Shanghai Pharmaceutical, tried to cover up the cause of the contamination—an attempt to save money by storing the leukemia drug in the same refrigerator next to another drug that is highly toxic. That same company, Hualian, is the sole manufacturer of the RU-486 abortion pill, which is sold in the United States and produced by a plant located an hour's drive from the facility where the contaminated leukemia drug was manufactured.[7]

Active pharmaceutical ingredients are the most dangerous and high-profile Chinese exports with safety problems. But many other Chinese exports also have proven to be dangerously defective. In the United States, the Baxter heparin recall was merely the latest in a series of highly pub-licized incidents involving toys, tainted toothpaste, and toxic pet food, which sickened or killed thousands of dogs and cats. In August 2007, Mattel recalled nearly a million toys made in China that were decorated with lead paint. In the past decade there has been a steady rise in product recalls almost wholly attributable to the corresponding rise of Chinese imports in that period.[8] The Consumer Product Safety Commission re-ported that 61 percent of the 473 products recalled in the United States in 2007 were manufactured in China. In Japan, food poisoning involv-ing poisoned dumplings from China's Hebei Province led Japanese food distributors to consider ceasing procurement in China.[9]

Inadequate Regulation of Drug Manufacturing in China

In May 2007, the former State Food and Drug Administration (SFDA) chief, Zheng Xiaoyu, was sentenced to death for taking $850,000 in bribes to facilitate the approval of a number of new drugs, including some that contained substandard or counterfeit ingredients. One tainted antibiotic that Zheng approved after receiving a bribe led to the death of ten people. Rather than inspiring confidence, however, Zheng's execution raises questions about whether China is really willing and able to institute the kind of thoroughgoing bureaucratic and institutional reforms necessary to assure the integrity of its drug supply chain.

Notwithstanding the headlong leap of the global pharmaceutical industry into manufacturing drugs in China, safety problems are serious, pervasive, and multifaceted. A year after Zheng's execution, Professors Wei Zhang and Xue Liu of the Guanghua School of Management at Peking University interviewed executives from both domestic and foreign pharmaceutical corporations, hospital executives, and officials from regulatory agencies.[10] What they found was alarming. A majority expressed concern about the bioequivalence of generic drugs. The specific reasons given for concern were inadequate technical standards during drug development, inadequate government capacity in reviewing the documentation during the drug approval process, and in rarer cases data manipulation during clinical trials.

In the area of manufacturing, Liu and Zhang's findings are even more alarming. They report that because of cost concerns many manufacturers do not follow China's good manufacturing practices (GMP) regulations, which are in any case already less exacting than U.S. GMP. Zhang and Liu, moreover, found problems with "incomplete, untimely or 'selective' accreditation, failure to update accreditation following equipment change, lack of compliance with accreditation protocol, and data manipulation." "In a few companies," Zhang and Liu report, "GMP software incompatibility and staff incompetence were additional obstacles." Moreover, they found that "problems with production protocol, often resulting from unsophisticated R&D, also contribute to inconsistent product quality."

How widespread are the problems in Chinese drug manufacturing? In the year following Zheng's execution, Zhang and Liu report, the SFDA revoked the GMP certificates of 128 manufacturers, suspended the production of 168 other factories, and issued warnings to 2,025 manufacturers. In all, the SFDA identified problems at 50 percent of the five thousand *known* drug manufacturing facilities in China.

Inadequate adherence to GMP is not the only challenge for China. The regulations themselves are problematic. GMP standards are not as rigorous as U.S. FDA standards either in regard to the active pharmaceutical ingredient (API) or the non-active excipients, the two components of any drug product (the final dosage form). Dr. Arthur Fabian, a pharmaceutical executive with over thirty years' experience, has inspected several Chinese API facilities, lectured at Chinese regulatory conferences, and worked with Chinese companies to assist them in meeting U.S. good manufacturing practices (GMP). Dr. Fabian reports that "at first blush there is a very reasonable correspondence between the subjects covered by Chinese GMPs when compared to those in the United States. With a few notable exceptions, the same topics are covered. The problem is one of specificity. The Chinese regulations tend to be so vague and general that they offer very little real direction or guidance on what steps to follow to assure the production of adequate quality API or Dosage Form. The 'What' is there, but the 'How' is virtually absent." Dr. Fabian notes that U.S. FDA regulators strike a reasonable balance between the "what and how" of regulations, developing them with enough specificity to be useful but retaining enough generality to allow the possibility of approaching the issue in a better way. "Admittedly finding this balance is not an easy task, but it is a necessary one if the GMP regulations are to really mean something," said Dr. Fabian.[11]

Dr. Fabian also identified three critical areas not addressed at all in the Chinese GMPs. Each of these three omissions creates major safety and quality risks. The first concerns the traceability of an API or dosage form. In China, according to Dr. Fabian, drug companies consider their suppliers a trade secret and thus there is not a system in place to identify the actual manufacturer should an API or dosage form begin to show adverse effects on patients. Under applicable U.S. and European manufacturing guidelines, each ingredient used in manufacturing drugs must be traceable to its source via the label, which must clearly identify the actual manufacturer.

A second major omission Dr. Fabian highlights is that the Chinese GMP regulations do not discuss subcontracting: "A U.S. or European pharmaceutical company may send staff over to China to inspect a facility. They might be totally satisfied with the quality systems of the plant. The problem is that the Chinese might think nothing of subcontracting out part of the work to another facility that has not been inspected. This would not meet European or U.S. GMPs, but Chinese regulations are silent about this issue."

A final area of significant risk in Chinese GMP, according to Dr. Fabian, is the lack of regulation of change control: "This is a major area of concern. Very often you might have a product approved by the FDA along with an approved process and location for manufacturing, but, after approval, you may have to change the process, or the site where it is manufactured, or the scale of production." Dr Fabian warns that "any of these changes might have an impact on the product's quality and in the U.S. there are strict procedures about informing the FDA about such changes and the requirement to demonstrate that the changes do not, in fact, have an adverse affect on the quality of the API or Dosage Form. There is no such change oversight in effect in China, so if there is a manufacturing change after an initial approval, there is no way of telling the effect this might have on quality."

Institutional Causes of Drug Safety Problems

China's drug safety problems also have deep-rooted institutional causes. Power over approving new drug applications is vested in the SFDA, a national agency that also reviews clinical trials and oversees manufacturing inspections.[12] But the SFDA lacks jurisdiction over the production and distribution of chemicals that often wind up as ingredients in pharmaceuticals in Western countries—a huge legal loophole that essentially leaves many manufacturers of drug ingredients unregulated and not required to meet even minimal SFDA standards.[13] Ostensibly, responsibility for product safety, including pharmaceuticals, is also vested in the General Administration of Quality Supervision, Inspection, and Quarantine and the China Fine Chemicals, Materials, and Intermediate Association. However, the existence of divided yet somewhat overlapping jurisdictions means there is often no agency in charge, and responsibility for drug safety falls between the cracks. For example, in October 2007, ABC News investigators contacted representatives of all three Chinese agencies to determine which one had jurisdiction over the case of tainted cough medicine that resulted in more than one hundred deaths in Panama and the scandal involving counterfeit infant formula that caused thirteen babies in China's Anhui Province to die from malnutrition. None of the three agencies would acknowledge having regulatory power over either of the incidents.[14]

The chaotic lines of authority in China's drug regulation regime must be understood as a manifestation of China's underdeveloped legal system. As discussed more fully in chapter 5, China lacks an independent judiciary that delineates lines of authority among competing political units. As a result, there is no clear demarcation of power among various governmental agencies and among national, provincial, and local governments. Moreover, there is almost always a complete lack of transparency in legal reform and rule making. In most cases, regulations become effective without prior public comment. Even after regulations become effective they are often not even published or available for review by affected parties.

In March 2007, the Chinese government announced that the SFDA would be subsumed under the Ministry of Health.[15] This reorganization did not specifically address the issue of overlapping jurisdiction, but a month later the government signaled its intention to close the chemical manufacturing loophole sometime in the future. However, the government's plan does not inspire much confidence that the loophole will be closed anytime soon. Yan Jiangying, deputy director of policy and regulation at the SFDA, has stated that "firms that do not have a permit from the SFDA to produce drugs or drug ingredients are strictly prohibited from conducting any drug-related business." In the same breath, however, Yan admitted that the SFDA has "never investigated a chemical firm, as it's beyond our scope."[16]

There are approximately eighty thousand chemical companies in China, and no one knows how many of these companies are involved in manufacturing drug ingredients. The SFDA has the power to inspect and certify any firm that identifies itself as a drug manufacturer. However, if a chemical company does not apply for certification, the SFDA does not have the power to prevent that company from selling active pharmaceutical ingredients and finished drug products domestically or internationally. As a result, drug ingredients from unregulated Chinese chemical factories flow unchecked into international commerce. Yan Jianling of the SFDA commented that such sales were "definitely against the law," but she has repeatedly stated in multiple public statements that her agency has "never investigated a chemical company. We don't have jurisdiction." Chinese manufacturers understand this perfectly well. As Bian Jingya, export manager for Changzhou Wejia Chemical Company, put it: "If you want to be regulated they will regulate you. If you don't want to be regulated, they don't."[17]

One has to wonder what is at the bottom of this regulatory weakness and confusion. As a formal legal matter, the SFDA's lack of jurisdiction over the manufacturing of drug ingredients by chemical companies can be easily fixed. Simply give the SFDA the power to regulate the manufacturing and sale of all drugs and active pharmaceutical ingredients. Given the technical ease with which this problem of jurisdiction can be fixed, several possibilities emerge to explain this anomaly. First, it might just be the underdeveloped nature of China's legal and regulatory system. Pharmaceutical manufacturing is not the only area where there are overlapping jurisdictions and regulatory gaps. Under this benign explanation, the government simply needs time to work out all the coordination issues at the national, provincial, and local levels.

A second explanation is less benign. Does it suit the Chinese government to allow pharmaceutical and chemical companies unfettered access to global markets? The pharmaceutical industry is a rapidly growing sector in China. As China seeks to move its economy away from low-wage manufacturing to higher-value-added production, the pharmaceutical and chemical industries are obvious candidates for strategic national champions. Slow-footed safety regulation serves as a crude form of "industrial policy," fostering growth in these industrial sectors. Moreover, many of these chemical companies are partially owned by local and provincial governments or by individual Communist Party members. For all these reasons, there appears to be little political enthusiasm or will to close such obvious and significant regulatory loopholes even though reasonable solutions are within reach. Corruption continues to be a major problem in China, particularly at the provincial and local level where companies can exert significant influence to block regulatory initiatives emanating from Beijing. "The mountains are high and the emperor is far away," according to a traditional Chinese saying. One Western pharmaceutical executive with longstanding experience in China cites this kind of corruption-based regional protectionism in China as a major impediment to the development of an effective drug regulation system.[18]

Another impediment to the development of an adequate and responsive drug safety regime in China is the absence of an effective and independent court system where civil litigants can obtain monetary compensation for injuries they or their loved ones suffered from defectively manufactured products. A more robust civil law system that will allow plaintiffs the ability to recover meaningful compensatory and punitive damages—whether for wrongful death, disabilities, or pain and suffering—from Chinese manufacturers and distributors will likely go a long way toward drug safety by creating stronger financial incentives for companies to think twice before unleashing something dangerous into the marketplace. While the law of negligence and product liability is an integral part of safety regulation in the United States and other developed nations, in China innocent consumers who have been injured by unsafe and adulterated products have very limited legal rights to exact compensation from responsible companies. Only time will tell whether civil law and the court system in China will evolve to offer greater protections and remedies to injured consumers. Thus far, the results are not encouraging. For example, the Chinese courts have refused to even hear the claims of the parents of the 300,000 children sickened by melamine-tainted milk. Instead, the government has been pressuring the plaintiffs to accept an out-of-court settlement offer from the milk producers.[19]

In sum, a number of governmental and industry factors contribute to the lack of safety assurance in China's drug industry. On the governmental side, there is a weak regulatory system with unclear and overlapping jurisdiction, gaps in coverage, inadequate resources, a weak tort litigation system, and corruption. On the industry side, safety is compromised by the lack of training and technical capacity, failure to follow global good manufacturing practices, a lack of a culture of safety and product quality, and downward cost pressures. Moreover, these factors characterize the five thousand companies that are identified as drug manufacturing companies. Conditions may be worse at the estimated eighty thousand firms currently classified as chemical companies that might nonetheless be manufacturing ingredients for the global drug industry.

What all this adds up to is a recipe for disaster—meager and inadequate resources to regulate a fragmented and diffuse industry. China's internal task in assuring drug safety is twofold—to build regulatory capacity and to reduce the need for it. At the moment the drug supply chain is so scattered among tens of thousands of small companies, including innumerable small mom-and-pop operations, all with limited resources and know-how when it comes to adhering to good manufacturing practices. As a result, there is a lot of policing to be done by regulatory authorities and limited resources with which to do it. As companies merge and economies of scale and scope are achieved there will be fewer companies that need to be regulated and those that are regulated will have more resources to invest in safety.

The short-term task for China is to increase the amount of resources devoted to policing. The long-term task is to encourage industrial consolidation so that fewer resources are necessary. This process of industrial consolidation will take decades to accomplish in China. In the meanwhile, regulatory resources will inevitably fall short of what is needed. As a result, it will be decades before production standards in China meet global safety standards. This should not be shocking to anyone. China is after all a developing country just three decades into the process of economic reform and market privatization. It is still an authoritarian country with a poorly developed legal system. It is unrealistic to expect that at this point in its economic and social history that it would have either the intellectual and technical capital or the regulatory sophistication to sustain a pharmaceutical industry that would supply the world with drug ingredients. Making T-shirts, running shoes, and toys is one thing. Making safe and efficacious drugs is quite another. China may eventually get to the point when it will have a world-class pharmaceutical industry. That time, however, is decades in the future. In the meanwhile, citizens of other countries should not be expected to be the guinea pigs in China's learning curve on manufacturing drugs safely. That is precisely what is happening now as the pharmaceutical industry has joined sneakers, T-shirts, toys, and electronics in the manufacturing "race to the bottom" in China. What the Western world seems very slowly to be waking up to is that in the case of toys (which are marketed to children) and drugs (which are inherently dangerous products) the causes of concern are not only labor rights and the exodus of good manufacturing jobs for workers. Lives are literally at stake when the global drug manufacturing embraces the "race to the bottom" imperatives of unregulated cost containment.

U.S. and European Efforts to Regulate the Safety of Drugs Manufactured with Chinese Ingredients

The FDA and its European counterpart, the European Medicines Agency (EMEA), have been slow to adapt to the globalization of active pharmaceutical ingredients. "Today the oversight arm of medicine agencies everywhere is seriously obsolete, broken, and unable to discharge its responsibilities and to cope with the rate of change," says Guy Villax, the chief executive officer of Hovione, a Portuguese-based pharmaceutical manufacturer and member of the European Fine Chemicals Group.[20]

As the heparin incident illustrates, unsafe pharmaceutical ingredients can potentially slip into the United States and Europe through superhighway-sized loopholes and gaps in the international drug safety regime. The Synthetic Organic Chemical Manufacturers Association's Bulk Pharmaceutical Task Force (BPTF) estimates that more than 80 percent of the Active Pharmaceutical Ingredients (APIs) used by U.S. companies to manufacture end product drug dosages are imported. Half of those imports, moreover, originate from India and China.

Despite the fact that the great majority of APIs are manufactured outside the United States, however, the FDA inspects less than 10 percent of the *known* pharmaceutical manufacturing plants in China and elsewhere in the world.[21] A U.S. Government Accounting Office study found that in 2007 the FDA inspected just 13 of the 566 plants in China that are certified by the FDA to export to the United States. Given that the Chinese SFDA has found problems at half of the plants it surveyed, this low percentage in itself represents a major threat to drug safety.

By law each U.S. plant must be inspected every two years, but the FDA inspects far fewer foreign plants. This legal anomaly may help to explain why the FDA's inspection resources have not to date been deployed in a manner that is anywhere near proportional to the places where APIs are today actually being manufactured. Struggling with limited budgets and manpower, FDA commissioner Andrew von Eschenbach admitted in congressional testimony that the FDA "must revamp our entire strategy, our entire game plan."[22] One possibility the FDA needs to consider is to seek legislative action that would allow it to deploy more of its limited inspection resources abroad.

One step the FDA has taken is to open a small office in China but, in addition to the grossly inadequate resources that will be located in China, there are many factors that stand in the way of such efforts assuring a level of manufacturing safety anywhere near the levels that one can expect in the United States. Obviously there is a language barrier. In addition, unlike in the United States and Europe where inspectors can enter manufacturing facilities without notice, FDA officials are not allowed to enter a foreign facility without advance notice and an invitation. Moreover, as troubling as the FDA's inability to properly inspect known drug manufacturing facilities might be, there is also the issue of chemical companies that remain completely unregulated in China and yet are still exporting pharmaceutical ingredients. Joseph Acker, president of the Synthetic Organic Chemical Manufacturers Association, a trade organization representing U.S. drug ingredient manufacturers, sums up the situation by observing that the "FDA is by default creating two different enforcement regimes. A domestic one, where manufacturers expect and receive a visit by a FDA official every two years, and a second one for outsourced APIs that are almost never uniformly inspected."[23]

European Union authorities have not done much better than the FDA. In the past, the European Medicines Agency (EMEA), which was established less than fifteen years ago, had been considered the "weak sister" of the older and better-funded FDA.[24] Under recently enacted laws, however, the EMEA received several new powers that exceeded that of the FDA, including the ability to demand safety studies from drug companies even after a product has gone to market and the authority to remove a pharmaceutical from the marketplace if clinical evidence shows it to be less efficacious than previously believed.[25] But in the past seven years the European Union—which like the United States also imports 80 percent of the key pharmaceutical ingredients that it consumes—inspected only forty active pharmaceutical ingredient production sites in China and India combined.[26] In congressional testimony in November 2007, Hovione's Guy Villax summed up how Europe's lack of inspections and oversight has encouraged the flow of substandard, fake, and possibly dangerous drugs into its borders. "It appears that even companies in China and India that have been blacklisted by Nigeria's health authorities [because] of their proven, deep involvement in exporting counterfeit medicines to that country, are still freely exporting [active pharmaceutical ingredients] to the E.U.," Villax testified. "The little evidence we have shows overwhelmingly that the E.U. system is broken and that using shortcuts has become a profitable business."[27]

Unsafe Trade: How U.S. Negotiators Bartered American Safety in Exchange for Access to Chinese Financial Markets

In May 2007, mindful of the gaps in China's drug regulation system, Health and Human Services Secretary Michael Leavitt began discussions with Chinese officials. In the first week of December, Secretary Leavitt boldly and inaccurately declared that "any country that desires to produce goods for American consumers needs to produce them in accordance with American standards—American standards of quality, American standards of safety."[28] Less than a week after this statement, U.S. negotiators signed a product safety agreement that fell far short of Leavitt's lofty rhetoric. The agreement requires Chinese drug producers to register with the Chinese government and obtain an export license before exporting to the United States. However, there is an absurdly fatal flaw to the agreement. It covers only ten products! The products covered by the agreement include human growth hormone; oseltamivir, an antiviral drug; and gentamicin sulphate, an antibiotic.[29] No other drugs or drug ingredients are covered. Thus under the terms of the agreement, Chinese companies that are exporting drug ingredients to the United States in all but the ten categories covered by the agreement are not required to be inspected by Chinese regulators. Moreover, the status of "chemical" companies remained unclear. As a Chinese negotiator admitted, "it is unclear which [chemical companies] can produce drug ingredients and which cannot."[30]

Less than a month after the agreement was signed the heparin incident shone a light on how contaminated active pharmaceutical ingredients manufactured in facilities that were not inspected by either U.S. or Chinese regulators could be exported to the United States and Europe. The agreement is a political and economic compromise that leaves the American public open to significant health and safety risks. One can only hope that China will be able to move quickly to shore up its regulatory capacity because, for now, the United States has proved unwilling to pressure its largest trading partner into speeding up its process. China's pharmaceutical industry continues to enjoy open access to the U.S. drug pipeline with an overall safety standard that, contrary to Secretary Leavitt's rhetoric, is far below what the United States is willing to tolerate from its domestic producers.

How did the U.S. trade negotiators conclude such a one-sided agreement that exposes American consumers to dangerous Chinese drug ingredients? The answer is that safety issues were bartered away in exchange for Chinese promises to open up participation in banking and securities investment. This was done in the context of the third meeting of the so-called U.S.–China Strategic Economic Dialogue where the U.S.

delegation was led by Treasury Secretary Henry Paulson. Even before the meeting began in Beijing in December, Wu Yi, China's highly experienced and shrewd trade negotiator, was intoning that U.S. concern over the safety of Chinese exports was injecting "disharmonious notes" into the U.S.–China relationship. Wu Yi dangled product safety as a bargaining chip for market access in banking and securities investment. Over a decade earlier in trade negotiations Wu Yi famously said that China was a "big piece of cake and those who come first would get the biggest slice." Secretary Paulson, a veteran of Wall Street but not nearly as experienced as Wu Yi in international negotiations, took the bait. He was all too willing to sacrifice the safety of American consumers for the sake of expanded financial investment in China. If American citizens wonder how it is possible that unsafe Chinese ingredients continue to flow unchecked into the drug supply, the answer is that when the subject last came up for negotiation, Secretary Paulson traded away the right to stop the flow of unsafe drugs in exchange for expanded access for the financial and banking industry.

So how should U.S. trade negotiators approach the drug safety issue with China? First and foremost, safety issues should be taken off the list of items that can be horse-traded. It should be made clear that no pharmaceutical ingredients can be imported into the United States unless the factories manufacturing those ingredients are registered with and periodically inspected by the FDA and follow manufacturing standards that are as good as U.S. GMP. The U.S. FDA should, moreover, have the right to inspect any plant manufacturing API for the U.S. market without prior warning as it does in the United States. If this seems overreaching it should be borne in mind that such unannounced inspections have already become routine in China for NGOs that monitor factories for labor violations. The U.S. FDA would not be expected under this system to be the ultimately responsible regulator. That responsibility would remain with the Chinese government. Rather, this is a "trust but verify" strategy that is intended to provide assurances that Chinese regulation is effective. Over time, as China develops an effective drug regulation regime, the FDA role in inspecting Chinese plants that export API can be scaled back. That day will, however, be sometime in the distant future and for now FDA efforts in China need to be quickly scaled up to catch up to what has already become a huge regulatory black hole.

Suppose the Chinese refuse to agree to such a drug safety pact? What recourse does the United States have? Thus far, Chinese officials have been unwilling to accept responsibility for the safety of their drug exports. This point was made explicitly after the heparin incident in a statement on the SFDA website that claimed "safeguarding the legality, safety and quality of raw materials imported for use in pharmaceuticals is the responsibility of the importing country."[31] The only way to dislodge China from such complacent irresponsibility is to link drug safety to trade law. There are a number of potential levers for doing so under existing international trade laws. Under relevant WTO provisions, for example, a nation has the right to restrict imports where "necessary to protect human...life or health." Moreover, the Agreement on Sanitary and Phytosanitary Standards (SPS Agreement) further articulates the principle that so long as a country bases its judgment on internationally recognized scientific standards, imports can be restricted for safety and health reasons. (Under NAFTA, the provisions allowing countries to adopt levels of safety protection as they see fit are even more forcefully articulated.)[32]

Based on the SPS Agreement, the United States would have a very strong case to ban all imports of drug ingredients from China unless China upgrades its regulatory practices. In other words, the United States should insist that the *only* drug ingredients that would be allowed into the United States would be those that are manufactured in FDA-inspected facilities. All other drug ingredients that do not have export licenses should be refused at the border. If Chinese negotiators express indignation at such a proposal, U.S. negotiators should match their indignation with equal indignation along with a reminder of the dozens of U.S. citizens who died and hundreds of others who fell ill from tainted heparin. This is one issue where the United States in negotiations with China needs to take a hard line. China's status as a developing country should not entitle it to special standards when it comes to the safety and integrity of the international drug supply. The message needs to be tough and unequivocal—improve safety regulation or lose the privilege of exporting drugs and pharmaceutical ingredients.

Some might argue that the policy I am proposing will increase the costs of drugs for U.S. consumers or slow down the drug pipeline. My answer is that it will and it should. The goal of finding the cheapest place in the world to manufacture drugs has reached a very dangerous point, particularly in the manufacture of generic drugs that now constitute the majority of prescriptions filled and are being sold for commodity-like prices in big discount stores such as Wal-Mart. As Hovione's Guy Villax says, "hyper-competition is causing generics to constantly look for lower costs and absent an effective floor set by regulators it is likely that we are moving at an accelerating pace to areas of unacceptable risk. However, generics are too politically correct for anyone to say that their quality is quite often inadequate and that no formal check exists to ensure that over time bioequivalence remains unaffected after years of change."[33]

The trade-off between drug safety and cost has been an issue in drug regulation for at least a half a century in the United States. Whenever Congress proposes a law or the FDA issues a regulation that attempts to assure drug safety, there is the potential for that regulation to raise drug costs. The difference in the case of manufacturing in China is that there is no democratic debate. When Congress considers a law or the FDA proposes a regulation, there is a public debate about its effects and the final result reflects a compromise that reconciles safety and cost considerations. In the case of pharmaceutical imports from China, however, a complete end run has been done around the carefully crafted, democratically enacted regulatory system. With no accountability and no public debate, the pharmaceutical industry has managed to essentially rewrite the U.S. drug safety laws by sourcing from China. This must be put to an end and done so quickly before a tragedy far greater than the heparin incident occurs. If drug companies want to manufacture in China they must do so in FDA-inspected plants according to GMP standards that are the functional equal of U.S. standards. Anything less is not only a grave threat to America's safety but also a cynical evasion of our democratic regulatory institutions. Free trade should be safe trade.

Corporate Responsibility for Assuring the Safety of Drugs Manufactured in China

In the wake of the highly limited and flawed bilateral trade pact signed in 2007, China's drug industry remains a significant danger to its own citizens and the rest of the world. At the moment, because of the limited resources and political will, neither Chinese nor Western regulators are able to safeguard the integrity of the drug supply chain. Given this regulatory void, the ultimate responsibility for safety in the drug supply chain falls squarely on the shoulders of pharmaceutical manufacturers and distributors. Some in the industry wishfully suggest that market forces will ultimately compel companies to cut back on the manufacturing of API in China. Brian Scanlan, the vice president of Wisconsin-based Cambridge Major Laboratories, observes that in the ten years that companies have been manufacturing drug ingredients in China that "the risks associated with manufacturing there are being more clearly defined and elucidated." Scanlan argues that companies are learning that "the development of active pharmaceutical ingredients and final dosage forms to support preclinical and clinical development is best done in the West, where there are tighter controls over intellectual property, faster development cycle times, and tighter control over development and manufacturing activities." Scanlan also believes that language and customs issues as well as a historically weak dollar in 2008 also are driving some global multinationals and biotech firms to return to Western supply sources over China and India.

However, other industry observers insist that, notwithstanding the safety and quality issues that have come to the fore, China will, in the near future, account for more than 75 percent of the API consumed in the United States.[34] The cost savings that can be achieved there are simply too attractive for pharmaceutical companies to pass up. Indeed, at this point some industry observers argue that the United States and Europe no longer have the capacity to manufacture drugs were production to shift back from China.

If the trend toward manufacturing API in China is indeed irreversible, then how should responsible companies behave when they source pharmaceutical ingredients in China? A few basic precepts should be kept in mind. First and foremost, it is important to understand that even though government regulatory standards are lower in China, corporate ethical standards must remain the same as in the United States and Europe. The safety issues arising from the outsourcing of drug manufacturing are fundamentally different in character from the labor issues that arise from outsourcing toys, running shoes, and apparel. In the case of worker rights issues, weak local protection of labor rights also places a moral burden on the brand-name companies to assure that their subcontractors adhere to certain minimal standards, for example, a minimum wage. However, it is not necessary, nor in fact would it be appropriate, to pay the same wages in China as in the United States. In the case of drug manufacturing, however, the standards of production must be exactly the same. Unsafe drug ingredients create significant negative externalities for public health in the rest of the world. Accordingly, it is reasonable to expect that when multinational corporations outsource to China to save money, they should not also attempt to evade the safety standards of their home countries. As one pharmaceutical executive commented, "regardless of where the ingredients or finished products are manufactured, drug companies bear ethical responsibility for the safety and efficacy of products sold in the United States. They need to manufacture according to the same standards in China as they do in the United States."[35]

As a practical matter, this principle would require that when they outsource to China multinational corporations must adhere to Western, not Chinese, good manufacturing practices, at least until such time as China offers a reasonable GMP alternative. Global companies outsourcing in China should not hide behind the watered-down regulation of drug manufacturing in China. "Unfortunately, the Chinese FDA is not the U.S. FDA and these should not be considered equal," says Brian Scanlan. "I've toured Chinese SFDA-inspected facilities operating to Chinese 'good manufacturing practices' and these would never pass muster in a U.S. FDA inspection."[36]

Pharmaceutical companies must also learn to accept responsibility and accountability for every link in the supply chain all the way down to the most basic ingredients. The accountability and responsibility must be accompanied by supply chain transparency to allow regulatory bodies to verify compliance with good manufacturing practices. One U.S. importer of Chinese-made ingredients, Chemwerth, claims to have twenty Shanghai-based employees who conduct "a full service audit program that mimics" the Food and Drug Administration's audit.[37]

Another element of responsible sourcing is to be realistic about how much cost savings can be achieved. Safety problems tend to occur when the price paid to suppliers is unreasonably low. Pharmaceutical executives often cite the possibility of achieving 40 percent savings over U.S. costs. One sourcing expert explained that "when you start paying below the real value of what you're buying, the suppliers have to cut on quality controls. They won't use the right, or more expensive, ingredients, and you are just asking for trouble."[38]

The manner in which Baxter initially handled questions about heparin is a good example of how not to behave. When the matter first came to light, it initially refused to identify its supplier.[39] When Baxter eventually did identify its supplier, Scientific Protein Laboratories, that company initially refused to identify its suppliers in China, claiming it was proprietary information.[40] It is nothing short of outrageous that these companies would think it is acceptable not to be proactively transparent about their suppliers when lives are at stake. What is especially galling about these tactics is that they were the very same ones initially employed by shoe and apparel companies a decade ago when they were asked by activists to reveal the factories where their goods were manufactured so that labor conditions could be monitored. It is extremely unsettling to realize that two seemingly reputable pharmaceutical companies, which deal with matters of life and death, are ten years behind sneaker and T-shirt companies when it comes to corporate social responsibility and transparency in their supply chain.

Responsible manufacturing in China must also take into account the extraordinary number of adulteration cases that have occurred in recent years. Whether it is melamine in milk or diethylene glycol in cough syrup or starch in anti-malarial drugs, Chinese raw ingredient suppliers have evinced a disturbing propensity to introduce cheap and dangerous substitutes into the supply chain. These contaminants are often difficult to detect through conventional product testing. It took, for example, almost a month of testing for the FDA to conclude that the contaminant found in the heparin recalled by Baxter was oversulphated chondroitin sulfate.[41] Given this kind of criminal intent by unscrupulous suppliers, what responsibility do responsible drug companies have? Because such deliberate contamination has happened so pervasively in China, one must ask whether it is advisable to manufacture there at all. If a company nevertheless does decide to manufacture there it cannot do so on the premise that such criminal acts are unexpected and unusual. On the contrary, a responsible company must practice an extremely high degree of vigilance and innovation in testing the purity and efficacy of its raw ingredients. It must develop and implement a state-of-the-art adulteration risk program. Any less will not only be unethical but it might also expose a company to legal liability for those who might suffer injury on the grounds of gross negligence in failing to act reasonably in light of the obvious dangers of contamination.[42]

A few words should be said about one class of drugs for which China has not yet become the default manufacturing hub. In the next decade, "large-molecule" biologics or biotechnology-derived drugs will constitute an increasing proportion of new drugs in development. The proteins and antibodies involved in biotechnology-derived products have a complex molecular structure that is much more elaborate than "small-molecule" drugs obtained by chemical synthesis. Furthermore, biologics are synthesized in living systems such as microorganisms and plant or animal cells. These living systems are very sensitive to changes in the manufacturing process. Such changes can adversely affect the nature of the end product and the way it functions in the human body. For biologics, it has been said, "the product is the process."

As demand for biologics increases around the world, expanding capacity will be a challenge for the biotech industry. In addition, pressure to reduce manufacturing costs is mounting. As a result, a growing number of established biotech and pharmaceutical companies are already outsourcing with contract manufacturers.[43] Dr. Elena Arvenitis, an experienced research scientist in pharmaceutical drug discovery, notes that "the issue with biologics is that it is much more difficult to establish unequivocally, by current analytical methods, that one biologic has the same safety and effectiveness profile as another without running clinical trials. Thus, avoiding batch-to-batch variation in manufacturing processes and abiding by good manufacturing practices is even more essential in guaranteeing the quality, efficacy, and safety of the end product."[44] Thus, although the ship has sailed with regard to API, any reputable pharmaceutical company should be extremely wary of achieving cost savings by manufacturing biologics in China. Indeed, the FDA should seriously consider being much more hands-on in deciding whether or not any biologics should be allowed to be imported from China until the country's regulatory capacity and sophistication reaches its full potential. Safe trade requires that the federal and state governments in the United States invest in developing the capacity and infrastructure for manufacturing biologics, thereby also creating good-paying jobs for skilled workers.

The Need for a Global Solution: Assuring
Drug Safety in Poor Countries

A final point that should be addressed concerns vulnerable people in the developing world. Thus far, I have focused on the threat posed by unsafe Chinese drug ingredients to rich Western nations. However, the Chinese drug industry poses an even greater risk to impoverished countries. Whereas the supply chain in the United States and Europe relies for the most part on reputable and well-established companies, the supply chain to poorer countries is a shadowy morass of transshipments and shell companies. As *New York Times* reporters Walt Bogdanich and Jake Hooker painstakingly uncovered in their Pulitzer Prize–winning investigative reporting, the counterfeit glycerin that killed 138 Panamanians passed through three trading companies on three continents. Not one of them tested for safety or efficacy. The certificate accompanying the shipment was repeatedly altered, eliminating the name of the manufacturer and the previous owner. The Panamanian government, which bought the counterfeit product and mixed it into the cough syrup that killed its own citizens, did not even know where the product came from or who made it. They had no way of knowing that the Chinese factory that manufactured and misbranded the diethylene glycol was not certified to make pharmaceutical products.[45] Assurance of a safe drug supply is not something that only the rich nations of the world deserve. Had the Panamanian government known where the drugs were coming from and that it had been adulterated, it surely would have refused shipment of the counterfeit product.

Although it may seem utopian at this stage, a reliable system of tracking the production, quality, and distribution of drugs is something that the poor and the rich alike have a right to expect. Dr. Henk Bekedam, the World Health Organization representative in Beijing, has commented that "this is really a global problem, and it needs to be handled in a global way."[46] A big step in such a global solution would be to develop a tamper-proof drug labeling system so that no matter where a drug or pharmaceutical ingredient is sold in the world, its source of manufacture will be known. Although this would not necessarily guarantee product purity or authenticity, it would create much greater transparency and disincentives for manufacturers to engage in shenanigans when they know they can no longer do so in anonymity. In the event of serious problems with the product, the information would also allow regulators to quickly identify companies in the supply chain and hold the responsible parties accountable.

The technology and regulatory infrastructure to create transparency and accountability in the supply chain has been slowly developing in the United States and Europe but it must be deployed worldwide. As early as 1992, amendments were made to the Prescription Drug Marketing Act that required each party (other than the manufacturer or authorized distributor) engaged in the wholesale distribution of a prescription drug to provide a "pedigree"—a statement of origin identifying each prior sale—to the buyer. In February 2004, the U.S. pharmaceutical industry informed the FDA that it would voluntarily implement an electronic tracking system by 2007, a goal that has yet to be achieved.[47]

Simple justice demands that every citizen of the world has the right to know what goes inside his or her body. Free trade must be safe trade. If there is to be free movement of potentially dangerous drugs and ingredients on a global scale, then there must be a global system and standard of safety that must accompany such commerce. Until such a global system of safety and efficacy accountability is implemented, the flow of chemicals from China will remain a grave and looming threat to global health and safety.

Looking to 2020: The Benefits of "Safe Trade" for China

In this chapter I primarily have been concerned with the issue of product safety from the perspective of the United States, Europe, and other countries outside of China. However, China also has a big stake in how foreigners approach the issue of product safety. By insisting on adherence to adequate safety standards, foreigners will help shape the future of China in several important ways. Most obviously, there will be inevitable spillover effects for Chinese citizens as their own products become safer. Even before hundreds of thousands of Chinese children were sickened by melamine-contaminated milk in 2008, consumer confidence in the food and drug supply had eroded due to the pervasively unethical practices of many suppliers. By working with Chinese regulators to establish world-class safety standards and practices, Western companies can help China find an economic path that combines growth with safety.

On a broader level, the insistence on high safety and quality standards signals to China that, notwithstanding its membership in the WTO and its attractiveness as a source of foreign investment, the country still has a long way to go before it can move up the value chain of products from T-shirts and sneakers to more sophisticated value-added manufacturing sectors, such as pharmaceuticals, automobiles, and aerospace. It sends the message clearly that if China hopes to move up in manufacturing class, an essential component must be reform of its legal and regulatory system. That is a tough-love message but it needs to be delivered for China's sake if it hopes to build on its past economic gains in a sustainable manner. It is in China's interest to understand that its long run of export-led growth in which safety issues have often been swept under the rug is fast ending. If China has any hope of moving up in manufacturing class to more value-added products, it must place greater emphasis on safety and quality. Indeed, this kind of value shift will also be critical toward developing an internal consumer market for Chinese-manufactured products. Chinese consumers deserve and will demand no less.

Conversely, there are significant dangers if foreigners fail to insist on adequate product safety standards. This could well foster a sense of Chinese "exceptionalism." Chinese leaders and businesspeople will come to believe that the rest of the world is so eager to invest in China and make money that it is willing to overlook bedrock values such as safety and product integrity. One must remember that Chinese citizens are just beginning to learn about what it means to participate in the free market. They live and work in a system where the market is poorly regulated, the legal system has many loopholes, and wrongdoing can be easily hidden from detection. The way that foreigners behave will help to shape the business ethics environment in China. If foreigners are willing to cut corners or look the other way on safety and quality in order to squeeze out more profit, Chinese businesspeople will come to think of such behavior as normal and acceptable. As China becomes a more and more important part of the global political economy in the coming decade, this would indeed be a dangerous and destabilizing message to be sending.

4

CHINA 2.0

Illusion and Promise behind the "Great Firewall"

"Are you ashamed?" Representative Tom Lantos bellowed at executives from some of America's leading technology companies. This was a notable low point for these executives from Cisco, Microsoft, Yahoo, and Google during the February 2006 hearing before the United States House of Representatives International Relations Committee. In rapid sequence, a parade of legislators from both political parties took turns excoriating U.S.-based Internet companies for their business operations in China. It was, however, the questioning by Californian Congressman Lantos, a Holocaust survivor, that stung the most. "Yes or no?" Lantos demanded. "Are you proud of it or ashamed of it?"

The Congressional hearing had been convened to investigate a state of affairs that outraged legislators and engendered considerable dismay among the American public: China seemingly had done the impossible—it censored the Internet, a feat former President Bill Clinton had likened to "nailing Jell-O to a wall." What was even more galling to the Congressional committee was that the fingerprints of foreign companies—and

American technology firms in particular—were all over a series of actions that ran counter to the bedrock principles of open and democratic societies. Cisco sold the networking equipment that security officials programmed to filter out undesirable websites and spy on the e-mail correspondence of political dissidents; Google, whose widely publicized corporate motto was "Don't Be Evil," had launched a Chinese search engine that filtered out websites using terms such as "democracy," "Tiananmen Square," and "Falun Gong"; Microsoft deleted the writings of Zhao Jing, a pro-democracy advocate whose blog appeared on the company's computer server located on U.S. soil. Search engine and online content destination Yahoo was the most reprehensible of all in the eyes of many; Yahoo executives revealed to the Chinese government the identity of journalist Shi Tao. As a result, Shi Tao was sentenced to prison for ten years for using a Yahoo e-mail account he had believed was anonymous.

The disappointment and dismay in the United States over Internet censorship in China continues to run deep for a number of reasons. First, China's heightened profile with regard to censoring the Internet shattered a widespread naïveté about the deus ex machina power of Internet technology to transcend borders and reshape traditional power relations. Many China observers clung to the belief that the Internet would ineluctably empower new global "netizens" to flourish in the face of even the most repressive regimes. Clinton's observation that censoring the Internet would be like nailing Jell-O to the wall reflected this belief. But it seems that nobody had considered the ease of actually controlling access to Internet content with a simple adjustment to a network switch here and tweaks to a search engine there. Suddenly, it became abundantly clear that governments were still in charge, and not only could control news and other information accessible over the Internet but also could pressure the companies providing that access into revealing heretofore private information—resulting in the identification, punishment, and silencing of those whose beliefs and communications did not conform with the state agenda. As much as Internet technology could empower and inform the public, it was now evident that the same technology could also be a tool in the hands of authoritarian regimes to prevent unfettered access, disseminate propaganda, manipulate public opinion, and control its citizenry.

A deeper cause for concern was that China's Internet censorship undermined the idea that economic reform was helping to push its political system toward greater openness, democracy, and respect for human rights. In 2000, when the United States Congress approved China's accession to the World Trade Organization, a key premise was that economic liberalization and trade would have a positive impact on democracy and human rights. The Internet was the trump card for those favoring economic engagement; surely, as Bill Clinton insisted, China's rulers would have little chance of controlling the open and democratizing effect of the Internet. When it became clear, however, that the Chinese Communist Party could and would censor the Internet, it cast doubt on the putative connection between economic and political liberalization. Expanding business ties and introducing advanced information technology to China was supposed to bring greater freedom and democracy to Chinese citizens; but how was this going to happen if the companies presumably charting the path for an open information society were actually in cahoots with an unrepentantly authoritarian government?

In this chapter I reexamine the potential of the Internet to transform Chinese society and politics in light of the government's prodigious censorship efforts. I offer a balanced assessment of both the promise and the limitations of China's Internet as a catalyst for social and political change. I also examine the behavior and moral responsibilities of foreign corporations. The key questions addressed include: Have these foreign companies done their "fair share" to protect the human rights of Chinese citizens? On balance, have they advanced or hindered the transformative power of the Internet? Have they done as much as they can and should to improve human rights for China's 1.3 billion citizens?

One extraordinary fact has been lost in the hubbub over the role of American companies in Chinese Internet censorship: the sheer magnitude and vitality of Internet usage in China. There can be no question that Chinese authorities intend to control access to the Internet and that they have been rather effective in doing so. However, it is important to appreciate that the Chinese government has also made a conscious decision to speed China into the information age. The state has invested tens of billions of dollars to build a fast, cutting-edge national Internet infrastructure. At the same time, it remains determined to control its people's activities on the Internet as well as to closely monitor information sharing among citizens. The paradoxical result has been what might be called a controlled explosion of information.

According to the China Internet Network Information Center, in January 2009 a record-breaking 298 million people (23 percent of the population) used the Internet in China, which exceeds the number of users in the United States or Europe.[1] To fully appreciate the degree of Internet penetration in China, one need only to compare it with India. In 2007, India had 30 million Internet users.[2] In other words, on a per capita basis, China had approximately *seven times* more Internet users than India. Given that India is a democratic country and China is an authoritarian one, this is a startling and counterintuitive statistic. Clearly, China has chosen to invest significant resources in expanding its citizens' ability to access the Internet whereas India has invested more sparingly. Part of this reflects the fact that in recent decades China has had a far greater economic growth rate than India and consequently has more resources to invest in technology. From a purely Chinese perspective, however, the policy of letting the Internet grow while still endeavoring to control it mirrors the broader balancing act the Chinese government has been performing since the beginning of the reform era—embracing free markets while maintaining political control.

In a very real sense, the Internet represents the front line in the ongoing debate as to whether those two goals can be simultaneously achieved. The Chinese Communist Party wants to maintain control over the Internet while concurrently hoping the Internet will catalyze economic growth. In the coming decade, these inherently contradictory goals will engender broad social and political challenges for China. How completely will it be able to control the political and social dynamism of the Internet? Conversely, can a censored Internet fuel economic growth, or will the government's heavy-handed control of the flow of information eviscerate the Internet's potential to increase prosperity?

Foreign companies will play a crucial role in answering these questions. Will dynamic, world-class companies such as Microsoft, Yahoo, and Google be part of the solution or part of the problem? From a moral perspective, how much can we reasonably expect these companies to promote Internet freedom in China? As I describe in this chapter, the record of foreign Internet companies thus far has been decidedly mixed. When financial profits coincided with social progress, these companies played a useful role in helping the Chinese government build the Internet infrastructure, thereby enabling Internet access for Chinese citizens. When, however,

human rights and free speech principles inconveniently clashed with corporate profits, these companies all too eagerly sacrificed moral principles
for economic gain. As we shall see in this chapter, eventually, when their
economic gains in China fell short of expectations, foreign Internet companies belatedly came to the realization that their long-term business prospects depend crucially upon the expansion of freedom and human rights in
China. These companies even joined together to draw up a set of voluntary
guidelines to govern their business practices in China and other nations
that restrict free speech. I conclude by assessing the moral adequacy of
these voluntary guidelines and considering whether they are likely to have
any meaningful impact on Internet freedom in China.

China 451: How China Censors the Internet

> There was a kind of fish that lived deep in the ocean. It did not use its eyes
> very often, since it was used to the darkness down there. So its eyesight
> degenerated gradually until one day it became blind.
>
> —Chinese blogger "Keso"

> I don't know if it's better to speak out or keep silent, but if everyone keeps
> silent, the truth will be buried. I don't want to be silent, even if
> everyone else shuts up.
>
> —Seventeen-year-old girl blogger "Ruyue"

China censors the Internet through a highly efficient, multi-tiered, and
multifaceted system that blocks its citizens' access to thousands of websites outside of China and shuts down offending websites within China.[3]
Through countless eyes, electronic as well as human, the government
monitors websites, blogs, and e-mail within China. The system involves
national, provincial, and local administrative agencies as well as state-of-
the-art technology and tens of thousands of individual censors. Perhaps
the most pernicious and effective part of the system is the pervasive self-
censorship it exacts from Internet companies and ultimately from users
themselves.

China's censorship system begins at its borders. There are approximately
nine Internet pipelines into China, three of them major ones—one in the
north near Beijing, another on the east coast near Shanghai, and one in
the south near Guangzhou. At each of these connections, the Chinese

government has programmed network "sniffers" that block access to objectionable foreign websites, such as Human Rights Watch, the BBC, the Huffington Post, or Amnesty International. In addition to blocking entire websites on a permanent basis, the censors can prevent access to selected foreign articles about sensitive subjects, such as Falun Gong or Tibetan independence. Governmental censorship is also highly responsive to current events. When video footage of unrest in Tibet became available on YouTube, China blocked Chinese users' access to the popular video-sharing site. The government also censors web posts by and about dissidents who have been imprisoned for their speech.

A Chinese citizen who attempts to access banned sites or articles will receive a message that says the connection has timed out. After trying—and failing—to reach such a site several times, the Internet user should recognize the subtle unstated message that she or he should not have been trying to access that site in the first place.

The switches making all this access blocking possible were originally supplied by Cisco, but today that technology is widely available. There is now even a Chinese supplier for this blocking technology: electronics company Huawei. Although very effective at blocking foreign websites, the technology behind the censoring process tends to slow down the Chinese Internet, in particular when users are accessing even permitted sites located on foreign servers, which must pass through the network "sniffers" at the border.[4]

Within China, the government polices online content by relying on a combination of individual censors, rumored to be in the tens of thousands, and on self-censorship. The government monitors and blocks blogs, chat rooms, and e-mail for discussions of sensitive topics. On the government payroll are countless individuals who spy on the online activities of their fellow citizens. One U.S. MBA student who did her undergraduate work in China reported that her classmates would receive financial rewards from the government for turning in fellow students to censors.[5]

The quasi-governmental Internet Society of China requires online content and service providers to sign a "Public Pledge of Self Discipline" that, among other things, requires them to refrain "from producing, posting, or disseminating pernicious information that may jeopardize state security and disrupt social stability."[6] In other words, the government subcontracts the day-to-day work of censorship to private Internet service providers

(ISPs), which in turn hire their own private corps of censors. Eager to please and unsure of how much is enough, these companies proactively shut down anything they fear might offend the government's sensibilities and will often block out more information than do the government censors and filters.

As with virtually all other social and political issues in China, regionalism is an important factor in Internet censorship. Most of the leading domestic and foreign websites, including Sohu, Sina, Baidu, Yahoo, Neteas, and Bokee, are headquartered in Beijing, where the local censoring authorities are especially vigilant. By contrast, one of China's most popular Internet portals, Tengxun, is based in Shenzhen near the Hong Kong border. The local authorities there are not as strict, and thus some reports blocked on sites registered in Beijing are available on sites registered in the south. Moreover, most of the private newspapers that are bolder in reporting news, such as *Nanfang Dushi Bao* (Southern Metropolis News) and *Minzhu yu Fazhi Shibao* (Democracy and Legal Times), are also based outside of Beijing.[7]

Chinese ISPs will regularly shut down blogs and chat room discussions about topics expressly forbidden by government authorities. A study conducted by Reporters Without Borders found that any attempt to post a discussion topic including any words even remotely associated with the Tiananmen Square massacre of June 4, 1989—such as "1989.6.4," "1989 student movement," "unrest," "rioting," "massacre," and "uprising"— produced the following message: "Your message could not be posted because of its undesirable content. You are kindly asked to correct it." An estimated four hundred to five hundred other words and phrases also trigger Internet filters, including "wave of resignations by party members."[8]

The self-censorship efforts of private Internet companies go beyond the stated requirements of the "Public Pledge of Self Discipline." Reporters Without Borders has detailed a shocking level of tactical coordination between government officials and Chinese-owned ISPs, including weekly meetings and daily government directives about sensitive topics that need to be monitored and suppressed. In the two-month period of May and June 2006, the Beijing Internet Information Administration Bureau issued seventy-four directives on matters ranging from banning news items from news sources "using sources of information that do not comply with regulations" to ordering that coverage of civil unrest in the southern village of Shanwei be limited to a short list of officially authorized news sources. Another directive ordered that "regarding the issue of unequal income distribution, please use articles from the Central Committee's main information mouthpieces and nothing else."[9] The degree of coordination between government and private censorship is so tight that the government essentially is using corporations as its agents for manipulating public opinion and behavior.

During the Tibetan protests in early 2008, the state used its media machine to publicly cast the Dalai Lama as a "terrorist" and aired stories about the suffering of ethnic Han Chinese at the hands of Tibetan rioters. Censors blocked all coverage of Tibetan grievances. Through this carefully orchestrated manipulation of information, the Chinese government was able to whip up nationalist frenzy and anger over pro-Tibet protests by foreigners.[10] Although it is not always possible, Chinese authorities would like to control news and information flow through the Internet to shape and control popular opinion in whatever manner suits them at the time. For example, as described in chapter 1, when nationalist fervor against the Olympic Torch protests in France threatened to spiral out of control, the government sought to calm the situation by ordering Chinese ISPs to shut down any online discussion of anti-French sentiments.

Beyond the censorship imposed by Internet providers is the strong hand of government repression, particularly for cases in which Chinese citizens attempt to use the Internet for overt political purposes deemed contrary to the Communist Party line. The international writers association PEN reports that thirty-eight writers are now imprisoned in China, many of them for posting forbidden material on the Internet. In December 2005, for example, Yang Tongyan was sent to prison for twelve years for promoting the China Democratic Party on the Internet.[11] Thirty-eight may not sound like a lot when dealing with almost three hundred million users, but it is enough to send a potent message to the countless others who might have otherwise been emboldened to express their opinions or to share information online.

The final, and arguably the most pernicious, level of thought control is individual self-censorship. As the typical user navigates the Internet and encounters external censorship by the government and ISPs, self-censorship eventually becomes the norm. At first, the Internet might seem like a cornucopia without limit with the promise of complete freedom to explore any topic. Over time, however, Chinese users become accustomed to the fact that there are sites they cannot visit and subjects they cannot discuss online. An attempt to access a banned site will result in an immediate cyber slap on the hand as the triggered censorship system will render the user's Internet connection unusable for a short while.

Slowly and in large measure unconsciously, users learn to avoid forbidden subjects and websites that might disable their computers or, far worse, bring them to the notice of the ever-watchful authorities. With their every search and post tracked, capable of being evaluated for political correctness at any time, most Chinese citizens eventually begin to shy away from accessing unauthorized news sources or discussing sensitive topics. China-watcher James Fallows has suggested that "what the government cares about is making the quest for information just enough of a nuisance that people generally won't bother." Rebecca MacKinnon, a professor at the University of Hong Kong, adds that "whole topics inconvenient for the regime simply do not exist in public discussion."[12]

In an interesting twist, the government has gone out of its way to allow unfettered Internet access to foreigners at some big hotels in major cities. In addition, foreign businesses can arrange, at some expense, to have a dedicated, that is, uncensored, connection to the World Wide Web. Indeed, without this kind of high-speed access, many foreign corporations in information-heavy environments such as banking and insurance would not be able to conduct basic business functions in China. For that reason, foreign companies lobbied hard with the Chinese government to make sure that they would be exempt from Internet censorship and allowed to deploy technological solutions that bypass the network "sniffers" at the Internet border.

Carving Out Limited Private and Public Spaces on the Internet

Despite widespread and heavy-handed governmental censorship, the fact remains that the Internet has expanded personal freedom and democracy in China and likely will continue to do so in the upcoming decade. To be sure, the vast majority of China's 298 million Internet users are not discussing politics or controversial social issues. Like their counterparts in the West, they mostly are exchanging e-mails about personal matters, looking up recipes, following sports and entertainment, and pursuing hobbies. It is striking, however, that Chinese users have so quickly embraced the idea of social networking and self-expression on the so-called Web 2.0. According to the China Internet Network Information Center, 118 million Chinese people use their phones to access the Internet and there were 162 million bloggers. This phenomenon will become even more pronounced in the coming decade as over half of Internet users in China are under the age of twenty-five and 70 percent are under thirty.

With hitherto few outlets for Chinese citizens to express themselves, dozens of MySpace.com imitators such as Mofile.com, Mop.com and WangYou.com are growing dramatically. Tens of millions of subscribers to such services are sharing music, videos, pictures, and writings. The self-censoring private operators of these social sites are very careful that their content steers clear of pornography and controversial topics. Despite these very real constraints, however, most Chinese believe—with justification—that there is greater room for free expression and creativity on the Internet than in traditional Chinese media. One survey found that 73 percent of Chinese Internet users between the ages of sixteen and twenty-five felt they could do and say things online that they couldn't in the real world. (Only 32% of U.S. users felt that way.)[13] To put it bluntly, as bad as censorship is on the Internet, it is nowhere near as complete and foolproof as censorship in the traditional media. Moreover, tens of millions of ordinary citizens now have the opportunity to express their thoughts and feelings in a public sphere, a concept unimaginable to their parents' generation. Twenty-eight-year-old Li Mengyang, a Beijing television producer, is a subscriber to WangYou.com where he has posted some of his own poems and stories. Li believes that Web 2.0 is a more creative medium than television "where some creative ideas can't make it" because of censorship concerns.[14]

Because of the growth of the Internet, the communication medium and the message are for the first time in modern Chinese history not originating within the government. Increasingly, citizens are using the Internet to publish information widely and as a platform for expressing opinions that may not be banned outright but nonetheless are critical of government conduct or inaction. Often government censors are caught flat-footed by the speed at which information disseminates over the Internet. For example, there was an online outcry over the government's preoccupation with the path of the Olympic torch rather than on helping victims in Sichuan, when that region was devastated by the nation's deadliest earthquake in more than thirty years.[15] Other times, the matter under discussion might not be controversial when it is first being discussed, but by the time the government censors catch on, the genie is out of the bottle, so to speak. Increasingly, Chinese citizens are accessing the Internet through their telephones and using text messages instead of e-mail, making it even harder for government censors to keep pace.

In many cases, discussions in Internet chat rooms spill over into the traditional media. In some instances, these online discussions even have led to systemic political change. One such area in which Chinese netizens have had a profound impact is the judicial system. In March 2003, for example, Sun Zhigang, a college-educated migrant worker who worked as a graphic designer, was beaten to death while in police custody in the southern city of Guangzhou after having been arrested for not carrying a required registration permit. A newspaper article in Nanfang Dushi Bao (*Southern Metropolis News*) about the incident was posted to various Internet bulletin boards and received widespread publicity that would never have been possible through traditional local print and broadcast media. Moreover, although the initial report appeared on an independent-minded newspaper's website, the story was kept alive in an informal, viral network of chat rooms, blogs, and bulletin boards. The government eventually attempted to curtail the Internet discussion, but only after the incident had received national publicity. One eulogy about Sun posted on the Internet said that "you were imprisoned because you would not be a pet animal or a slave."

Eventually, Sun Zhigang's killers were brought to justice. Six police officers and officials were jailed for their role in Sun's death and two fellow inmates were sentenced to death. But the impact went far beyond this single case. The Sun Zhigang incident was an important factor leading to the government's scrapping of the entire "Custody and Repatriation" system under which three million migrant workers were being held each year in 800 detention centers. Xiao Han, a Beijing-based legal scholar who petitioned China's National People's Congress to ban Custody and Repatriation, said at the time that "this case has become a national event. The government has no choice but to address it."[16] In a sobering coda to the Sun story, however, Southern Metropolis News's outspoken editor Cheng Yizhong and three others were arrested soon after exposing the Sun case for alleged financial irregularities and corruption. Though eventually Cheng was acquitted, two of his colleagues landed in jail. The government's heavy-handed crackdown on the highly respected, profitable, and innovative Southern Metropolis News sent a chill throughout the Chinese journalist community.[17]

Another example of the impact of Internet activism on the legal system had all the elements of a Gothic novel. In 1994, She Xianglin was imprisoned for murdering his wife, Zhang Zaiyu, who had disappeared without a trace. A badly decomposed body was found and presumed to be his wife. She Xianglin confessed to the murder after being tortured by police in Hubei Province in central China. It turned out, however, that Zhang Zaiyu was living with another man and a child in the coastal province of Shandong. This only came to light in April 2005 when Zhang was spotted by a neighbor in Hubei where she had gone to surreptitiously gaze from afar at the daughter she had had with She. As in the Sun Zhigang case, the news of her reappearance first appeared in a local newspaper, but it quickly spread to the Internet where it was widely publicized. "I only wanted to sneak a peak," Zhang told the Chinese media. Eventually, the innocent She was released and paid compensation by the Chinese government.[18]

As in the Sun Zhigang case, the She Xianglin case was a catalyst for system-wide legal reform. The concern over forced confessions led to a new rule that China's Supreme Judicial Court would review all capital cases in open court. It is notable that in both these instances, it was the combination of the Internet and the privately owned and independent-minded newspapers that uncovered and publicized the facts that became the basis for change in the legal system. Based on cases such as those involving Zhigang and She, Columbia University law professors Benjamin Liebman and Tim Wu have argued that "the growth of investigative journalism in China, in particular among the market-driven newspapers that developed throughout the 1990s, combined with the Internet, is resulting in much greater attention to law and the legal system than at any prior point in Chinese history."[19]

Online blogging has also become an innovative engine for social and political change in China. The 162 million bloggers on the Chinese Internet occupy a vibrant social space. A visitor to some of the thousands of blog-hosting sites, such as bokee.com, will find vigorous exchanges of facts and opinions about controversial social issues such as domestic abuse, homosexuality, HIV/AIDS, and the death penalty. Those discussions often venture into areas with significant political implications. Sometimes information banned from major Chinese news websites finds its way into the Chinese blogosphere. In May 2008, for example, Internet blogs galvanized the public outrage that spurred the central government to step up earthquake relief efforts in Sichuan.[20] Despite the government's prodigious effort to censor blogs, the medium itself is too informal and fast moving to control fully. In May 2007, for example, farmers in the Guangxi Zhuang Autonomous Region rioted against government officials to protest China's one-child policy. Newspaper commentary on the riot was banned from official media; however, a Hong Kong–based *Yazhou Zhoukan* news report about the riots was republished in a blog on bokee.com.[21] Another blogger on bokee.com known as "Abang" published several commentaries critical of the government's one-child policy.[22]

For hundreds of millions of Chinese citizens, the Internet—the blogosphere in particular—has become a source of information that would not be accessible through traditional print and broadcast media that are far simpler to control and censor. Xiao Qiang, a veteran of the 1989 Tiananmen Square protests and now a professor at Berkeley's journalism school, observes that "Bloggers are quick to find euphemisms so that they can continue conversation despite keyword filtering. And most blogs have so many entries that it is easy for an individual to post an occasional provocative comment without being detected."[23] Rebecca Mackinnon cautions, however, that while "there is indeed a vastly larger space for public discourse on matters of public concern than existed a few years ago ... that space has limits."[24]

A dynamic example of how the Internet facilitates social and political activism is the online China Water Pollution Map (found at ipe.org.cn), started by investigative journalist-turned-activist Ma Jun. Estimates are that 70 percent of China's rivers and 90 percent of the shallow aquifer in urban areas are polluted to dangerous levels. The situation in the countryside is even worse. According to Ma, 300 million peasants have unsafe drinking water. Ma compiles his information from a variety of government, NGO, and independent newspaper sources and through the use of digital mapping, allows visitors to survey water quality, monitor pollution discharges, and track pollution sources. Ma is quite explicit about how he expects his website to inform public opinion and spur environmental activism. He says that "to protect water resources we need to encourage public participation and strengthen law enforcement. In some places, polluting factories and companies are being protected by local governments and officials. The public needs to take part in water monitoring and management if the situation is to improve. The first step to get the involvement of the public is to inform them."[25]

One of the boldest features of Ma's China Water Pollution Map is the naming and shaming feature aimed at corporate polluters. More than 2,500 companies have been identified by Ma as polluters. "Up to now," says Ma, "companies haven't felt much pressure from the public regarding their environmental performance....I hope we can get to the position where, one day, companies will explain to the public what toxic and harmful chemicals they use in their operations, and what measures are being taken to combat their harmful effects." Ma's Internet activism against corporate polluters has achieved results. To date, thirty companies, mostly multinationals, have approached Ma about being removed from the list. Ma says he will remove the polluting companies from the list if they agree to fix the problems identified and accept an independent environmental audit.[26]

To be sure, there are distinctive factors enabling Ma to carve out a safe space in environmental activism. His stance is in accordance with the goals of powerful government allies such as Prime Minister Wen Jiabao, who has been personally involved in pressing for environmental reform. As a result of this government support, the number of environmental NGOs in China has risen from 50 to 3,000 in just five years.[27] However, in a pattern familiar in China, the sentiments of the central government have met with stiff resistance at the local level where corruption and the desire to attract investment thwart enforcement of environmental regulations. In this national versus local stalemate over law enforcement, Ma and other activists are finding a voice on the Internet and playing a critical role in promoting political and social change. Ma and his water pollution map might not be an image as dramatic as that of student protesters in Tiananmen Square hoisting the Goddess of Democracy, but it is emblematic of a new kind of social activism and citizen participation in China that is squeezing through the cracks in China's censorship system, focusing on specific issues, and taking advantage of the broadcast power of the Internet to achieve pragmatic gains.

Some Chinese citizens are becoming so resentful of the yoke of censorship that they are speaking out and challenging the system in courts. Du Dongjing, a thirty-eight-year-old information technology engineer in Shanghai, sued a branch of China Telecom for contract violations when it shut down his website, which marketed personal finance software. "I believe that with the help of today's Internet, and the mood of the public, I can win this case," says Du. "I can even make a contribution to improving Chinese democracy." Internet activist Yuan Mingli goes so far as to predict that the censorship system will fail because "people's hearts have changed.... China cannot be completely disconnected to outside world anymore."[28]

How Foreign Companies Help Censor the Internet

The future of the Internet and the contribution it can make to democracy and human rights in China will be in the balance in the coming decade. There is a tectonic social and political struggle in progress: On one side, government censors are determined to keep the Internet under control; on the other side is a motley and robust array of ordinary Chinese citizens finding and expanding civic and public spaces within the gaps of the censorship system. How this struggle will turn out is far from determined.

The situation in China demonstrates there is nothing inevitable about the transformative power of the Internet. Conversely, however, there is nothing inevitable about the ability of the Communist Party to control it. The crucial factors that will determine the outcome of this struggle for the soul of the Internet include the determination and creativity of Chinese citizens and the degree to which private companies choose to cooperate with the Chinese government. As we have seen, despite the government's efforts at silencing dissent, the Internet has emboldened and empowered a new generation of activists who are disseminating information and working, often at great personal risk, for social and political change. What role will private Internet companies play in this struggle? If one looks at the behavior of Chinese-owned Internet companies, the answer is not very encouraging. Chinese-owned ISPs are both eager to grow and afraid of retaliation. They are interconnected through personal relations and economic interests with the government in ways that are not immediately transparent to foreign observers. As a result, Chinese-owned and -operated companies have embraced their censorship roles with a disconcerting relish. In fact, it was rumored that in 2002, when Baidu had a 3 percent share of the search engine market and Google had a 24 percent share, it was Baidu executives who complained to the Chinese government that Google's search engine was allowing Chinese citizens to access hundreds of sensitive sites that were being blocked by domestic companies.

It is in the context of this grand social struggle over Internet freedom that one must assess the role and moral responsibilities of foreign companies such as Google, Yahoo, and MSN (Microsoft's portal). In the coming decade, these corporations potentially can play a crucial role in unleashing the power of the Internet to expand freedom and the flow of information in China. Before being hauled in front of Congress to testify in 2007, however, U.S. Internet companies displayed little strategic vision or moral courage. Google, Microsoft, and Yahoo all took what could be regarded as minimal or cosmetic steps to mollify the impact of their self-censorship in the Chinese market, in the process capitulating to the government's censorship demands almost as fully as Chinese companies.

Google launched google.cn, a Chinese search engine that filtered out websites using forbidden terms such as "democracy," "Tiananmen Square," and "Falun Gong." Google did take some creative steps to mollify the effects of its self-censorship. The company set up a computer within China and identified the websites and subjects censored by the government at the Internet border. Google then censored only those subjects. Google's self-censorship is, at least in theory, less intrusive than that of local companies who might censor more broadly to make sure they don't run afoul of the government.

Google took several other palliative steps. When it blocked access to a site, it provided a notice to users: "These search results are not complete, in accordance with Chinese law." The company also declined initially to introduce e-mail service or host blogs in China because it believed these would require it to engage in even more censoring and repressive behavior.

Some aspects of Google's actions and explanations seem on their face to be disingenuous. The most patently absurd claim is that Google was not in

China to make money. Google founder Sergey Brin told *New York Times Magazine* reporter Clive Thompson that going into China "wasn't as much a business decision as a decision about getting people information. And we decided in the end that we should make this compromise."[29] With nearly 300 million Internet users in China, it strains credulity to believe that Google was motivated solely by "getting people information." Google's business model and profits are driven primarily by the number of people who use its search engine. By far its best chance of global growth is in China. If we are to seriously consider Google's attempts to justify its self-censorship, the company needs to come clean about one thing: Google *is* in China to make money.

Microsoft has also been deeply complicit in China's Internet censorship. It deleted the writings of Zhao Jing, a pro-democracy advocate whose blog appeared on Microsoft's MSN Spaces, which was located on a computer server located on U.S. soil. Chastened by the uproar over its actions, Microsoft's general counsel Brad Smith announced that the company would revise its policy in two respects. First, it would shut down a blog only if it received a "legally binding" notice from a government body. (Microsoft had removed Zhao's blog simply upon being asked informally by a Chinese official.) Second, it would remove the blog from viewing only in China and would allow people outside of China to view it. Mr. Smith averred that Microsoft needed to be "forthright and principled in the way we address issues like this."[30] The bottom line, however, is that Microsoft continues to operate a service available in China that will censor blogs—even those on U.S. servers that comport with U.S. law—if the Chinese government deems them to be too politically controversial.

Yahoo was the first major Internet company to enter the Chinese market. In 2002, it signed the "Public Pledge on Self Discipline," which to date Google and MSN have not done. As mentioned earlier, in 2005 journalist Shi Tao was sentenced to ten years in prison after Yahoo identified Shi Tao to Chinese authorities as the owner of an e-mail account that Shi Tao believed would be anonymous. Shi Tao was accused by the government of leaking "state secrets" to a pro-democracy website. This "state secret" was a memo that the state propaganda machine had sent out to Chinese journalists containing instructions on how they should suppress any mention of protesters, pro-democracy sentiments, or activist groups during an upcoming anniversary of the 1989 Tiananmen Square uprising. Yahoo claimed it did not know the actual purpose of the government's request, and Yahoo general counsel Michael Callahan also claimed that Yahoo did not have "day-to-day" operational control of its China operations because in 2005 Yahoo purchased a 39 percent stake in the Chinese firm Alibaba.com and merged all of its China operations into Alibaba. Yahoo's attempt to hide behind a thin veil of corporate ownership would appear to be a particularly cynical and transparent attempt to avoid its human rights responsibilities, particularly in light of the fact that the company values its investments in China and Japan collectively at $12.5 billion or more than a quarter of its overall valuation. (Early in 2008, the company rejected as inadequate a $44.6 billion offer from Microsoft.)[31] The company's efforts to evade accountability are not helped by Alibaba's CEO Jack Ma, a colorful character who may have set some sort of unofficial world record for pithy verbal obliviousness to corporate social responsibility when he told the New York Times Magazine: "Anything that is illegal in China—it's not going to be on our search engine. Something that is really no good, like Falun Gong? No! We are a business! Shareholders want us to make the customer happy. Meanwhile, we do not have any responsibilities saying we should do this or that political thing. Forget about it!"[32]

Human Rights Responsibility: Comparing South African Apartheid with Chinese Internet Censorship

All three of these U.S.-based Internet companies cited the need to follow Chinese law as their initial justification for practicing self-censorship. Mary Osako, a Yahoo spokeswoman, summed up this point of view when she said that "just like any other global company, Yahoo must ensure that its local sites operate within the laws, regulations and customs of the country in which they are based."[33]

The notion that one should "do in Rome as the Romans do," following local customs and laws, is for the most part a sensible idea; when corporations based in one country establish operations in another sovereign nation, they presumptively agree to be bound by that nation's laws. Moreover, a businessperson who wants to be successful in another country would do well to understand and follow not only the letter of the law but also the customs, mores, and even etiquette of that society. In recent decades, however, multinational corporations have been forced to consider the moral limits of this idea.

The apartheid laws of South Africa vividly illustrate that the law, customs, and mores of a country lose their presumptive validity in rare cases when they would require companies to violate fundamental human rights. Should one have done in "South Africa as the South Africans do" during the reign of apartheid? Should multinational corporations have discriminated on the basis of race in South Africa just because South African apartheid law required it? The idea that people should not suffer discrimination in employment, housing, education, their use of public facilities, and other matters on the basis of race is an example of a human rights norm that trumps local law and custom. It does not matter that the South African government duly passed and fought to uphold apartheid laws. Those laws were in conflict with the fundamental human right not to be discriminated against on the basis of race. A similar principle is at stake in the case of Internet companies in China. Article 19 of the Universal Declaration of Human Rights provides that "everyone has the right to freedom of opinion and expression. This right includes freedom to hold opinions without interference and to seek, receive, and impart information and ideas through any media and regardless of frontiers."

To call something a "human right" is to say that it imposes duties upon others to honor that right.[34] At a minimum, it imposes a duty not to violate that right or assist someone else in violating that right. The rights of freedom of opinion and expression and the rights to seek, receive, and impart information as enunciated in Article 19 of the Universal Declaration of Human Rights impose a duty on the Chinese government not to censor the Internet. Private companies operating in China have a duty not to assist the government in censoring the Internet. In certain circumstances, the existence of a human right imposes a duty not only to avoid violating or assisting someone else to violate a human right but also a separate duty to take proactive steps to honor or promote the right in question. As we shall see, this proactive duty also applies to Internet companies in China.

Internet companies in China face difficult choices similar to those faced by companies operating in South Africa under apartheid. One option is to leave because it is impossible to conduct business without violating human rights. Most foreign corporations in South Africa chose this option after the global spotlight fell on the issue of apartheid. Alternatively, they could stay and attempt to conduct their business without discriminating on the basis of race. Companies that wanted to stay in South Africa and avoid being complicit in human rights violations did so by following the "Sullivan Principles" outlined by the Reverend Louis Sullivan of Philadelphia. Most large multinational companies, even most of those that originally signed the Sullivan Principles, chose to leave South Africa. The twenty-five or so companies that stayed and followed the Sullivan Principles agreed to follow race-neutral precepts in their business operations in civil disobedience to the apartheid laws. They also pledged to publicly press for the release of Nelson Mandela and the dismantling of the apartheid regime.

One crucial difference between doing business in China and doing business in South Africa is that every company in South Africa had to make a moral decision about apartheid. A company that stayed in South Africa had to either obey the law and practice racial discrimination or break the law and treat all people equally regardless of race. A company would either be complicit in human rights violations or it would have to break the law. There was no neutral ground. By contrast, in China it is possible for most foreign companies to go about their business without being outwardly complicit in human rights violations. For brand-name companies whose subcontractors employ sweatshop labor, there is a potential issue of complicity in labor rights violations. However, these companies can avoid participating in the violation of worker rights by requiring their subcontractors to adhere to a workplace code of conduct that respects the basic rights of workers. As we saw in chapter 2, there are many problems and issues with the integrity of the system that has emerged to monitor adherence to such codes. Nonetheless, it is at least theoretically possible for multinational corporations to subcontract manufacturing in China without violating the rights of workers. Moreover, these companies can do so without, as in the case of multinationals in South Africa, violating any laws and practicing civil disobedience.

The situation facing Internet companies in China is similar to the situation that faced companies operating in South Africa. Internet companies cannot respect the basic rights of Chinese citizens to receive and transmit information without directly violating Chinese law. Just as in South Africa, they have a stark choice. Obey the law and violate basic human rights, or honor those basic human rights and practice civil disobedience. The Chinese party-state does not, however, lightly regard civil disobedience. There are many Chinese Internet companies that provide the same services that Google, MSN, and Yahoo do. If any of these foreign companies were to refuse to participate in censorship, the government would very likely deny them a license to operate in China. Thus, as a practical matter, Western Internet companies cannot remain in China and remain morally pure. If they stay in China they will be called on to aid and abet criminal crackdowns on ordinary citizens trying to convey opinions or pass on factual information that the government would rather suppress. Foreign ISPs must engage in what Georgetown business ethicist George Brenkert calls "obedient complicity," which "would occur when a business follows laws, regulations, guidelines, or expectations of a government to act in ways that support its activities that intentionally and significantly violate people's human rights."[35] The serious and repeated "obedient complicity" in human rights violations that Internet companies must engage in to operate in China raises the question of whether they should be there at all.[36]

Moral Compromise or Compromised Morals?

The stark reality facing Internet companies in China is that they will unavoidably have "dirty hands." There is no way to operate in China without compromising and violating basic human rights principles. It is impossible, in other words, to remain in China and be morally pure. Is there any moral justification for foreign Internet companies to stay in China if the only way to do so is to be complicit in human rights violations?

In testimony before Congress, Google's representative, Vice President Eliot Schrage, attempted to justify the company's actions by saying that it offers a "better" service in China than any of its competitors.[37] In essence, Google argues that the evil it does in China is outweighed by the good. Note that this consequentialist argument does not dispute that Google is "doing evil." It simply asks us to accept the evil because of the good the company is doing. This is an argument that might have some validity if "better" meant that foreign Internet companies were providing a service that would allow Chinese citizens to view websites that other Internet providers in China are censoring. There is, in fact, some evidence that Google's service is less censored than at least some other providers in China. According to a study by Human Rights Watch, "Chinese Internet users have access to significantly more information with Google.cn and the censored MSN operating in China. However, it appears that Yahoo is censored at approximately the same level as Baidu, the domestic search engine leader."[38] Does the resultant good enabled by Google's and MSN's presence outweigh the evil they do by censorship? The best case that can be made is that Google and MSN enable Chinese citizens to view materials they might not otherwise have access to if these companies withdrew from China. Based on the Human Rights Watch analysis, however, Yahoo's self-censorship cannot be justified under any circumstances. It censors as much as domestic companies, and more than it needs to, in order to be allowed to operate in China. In no sense do Chinese citizens have access to better Internet service as a result of Yahoo's presence. Thus, Yahoo's presence in China cannot be morally justified even if we use a moral standard of simply doing more good than evil.

So Google is not morally pure, but on balance the right to information is better served by its presence than if it were to withdraw from China. Any potential moral justification for the company's continued operations in China must rest on the details of how much more information is available on Google.cn relative to its domestic counterparts. If the difference between Google results and domestic search engine results is negligible, then it would not justify the company's continued presence in China. If the difference was significant, then the moral argument for staying would be stronger.

If Google censors only as little as it is required to do so in order to retain its license to do business in China, isn't this as much as we can reasonably expect from the company? After all, Google has responsibilities not only to Chinese citizens but also to its shareholders, many of whom expect the company to maximize its profits. It is perhaps these conflicting responsibilities between profits and human rights principles that Sergei Brin had in mind when he said that "in the end we decided we should make this compromise." Can such a compromise be morally justified?

George Brenkert argues that when companies are confronted with difficult and unavoidable choices between being morally pure and remaining loyal to their shareholders, "moral compromise" is permissible so long as the companies take other actions that strive to "mitigate and reverse" what they are currently doing.[39] As we have seen, Google has already taken some steps to mitigate the harm it causes to Chinese citizens. Unlike domestic search engines such as Baidu, where censored sites elicit a nondescript error message, Google informs Chinese citizens when it is censoring a site. It also initially declined to offer e-mail and blog-hosting services so as not to be put in the position of having to shut down blogs, spy on e-mails, or be used by the government to ferret out political dissidents. This intentional self-limitation of the services it would normally provide has no doubt significantly affected the company's profits in China. It is difficult to fault Google on the grounds that they could have done less censoring and still remained in China. Indeed, the company seemed quite diligent about avoiding business that would involve it too deeply in human rights complicity and mitigating its actions that did compromise moral principles. Google—the company that had vowed to "do no evil"—seems in China to be following a revised and somewhat less catchy corporate motto: "do more good than evil, try to avoid doing a lot of evil, and do no more evil than is necessary." To some this might represent an insufficiently idealistic goal to which to aspire. Nevertheless, Google does seem to have tried not to wholly abandon its ideals when they smacked up against the reality of doing business in China.

What about Microsoft and Yahoo? For them the moral issues are a good deal murkier, because, in addition to running a search service similar to Google, they also made a business decision to offer broader-based services in China. By hosting blogs and providing e-mail service, MSN and Yahoo have involved themselves more deeply in complicity with China's censors. Microsoft and Yahoo must shut down blogs, censor chat room topics about politically incorrect subjects, and even occasionally inform the government of the identity of citizens who use their services for legitimate political speech deemed illegal by the Chinese government. In short, because their involvement in censorship is much more extensive than Google, they do considerably more evil. Do they correspondingly do more good as well? That is highly doubtful. There is little evidence that the non-search functions of Yahoo and Microsoft enable any greater level of free speech than is possible on domestic Internet companies. As we have seen, Microsoft has already changed its policy to require that it would shut down a blog only if it received a "legally binding" notice from a government body, and that it would remove the blog from viewing only in China, allowing people outside of China to view it freely. At the end of the day, however, if the Chinese government formally requests Microsoft or Yahoo to shut down a blog, it will do so. Based on the standard of "moral compromise"—that it is acceptable to stay in China if one "does more good than evil, tries to avoid doing a lot of evil, and does no more evil than is necessary"—it is hard to make the case that the operations of Microsoft and Yahoo can be morally justified. Certainly, it is much harder to make the case for them than it is for Google.

The Duty to Promote Internet Freedom

Can we expect more from Internet companies than to "do more good than evil, try to avoid doing a lot of evil, and do no more evil than is necessary"? Is it practical to expect that foreign ISPs will take tangible steps to combat censorship in China? This sort of proactive promotion of human rights values was a central part of the Sullivan Principles. Companies adhering to the principles were expected not only to reject the practice of apartheid in their own operations; they were also expected to actively work "to eliminate laws and customs that impede social, economic, and political justice." Similarly, Human Rights Watch has called on Internet companies in China to "lobby and attempt to convince the Chinese government and its officials to end political censorship of the Internet." Are Internet companies morally required to engage in such proactive campaigns against Internet censorship? If so, what might be the most effective way to conduct such a campaign, by lobbying the Chinese government or by other means? To answer these questions it would be useful to apply the "Fair Share" principles of corporate responsibility for human rights outlined in chapter 1.

The Fair Share principles tell us that in considering whether corporations have a duty to promote human rights, three factors should be taken into account: (1) the relationship of the corporation to the human rights victims; (2) the potential effectiveness of the corporation in promoting human rights; and (3) the capacity of the corporation to withstand economic retaliation. When one applies the first criterion, the relationship of Internet companies to the human rights victims could not be more direct. It is their customers who are being deprived of their right to receive and transmit information and to freely express their opinions. The relationship is even deeper because Google, Microsoft, and Yahoo are directly involved in censorship, and it could be said that Yahoo and MSN have betrayed their Chinese customers. It is difficult to imagine a circumstance in which there would be a stronger proactive moral duty to attempt to improve human rights conditions. Indeed, the case for such a duty is even stronger here than it was in South Africa. There, a company that faithfully followed the Sullivan Principles did not itself practice apartheid. Here, by contrast, all of the Internet companies to a greater or lesser extent have dirtied their hands by directly and actively participating in some form of censorship. Moreover, the duty to promote human rights in this instance is not a general one; it concerns a very specific cluster of human rights issues having to do with censorship and free speech on the Internet. These are issues that go to the heart of the core values of these companies. If we cannot expect an Internet company, which is institutionally committed to providing the highest level of information services for its customers, to speak out against censorship, then from whom else could we ask that?

The final two criteria of the Fair Share theory concerning effectiveness and ability to withstand retaliation raise a host of difficult considerations. If foreign Internet companies attempted to raise human rights issues with the Chinese government it is unlikely that they would be effective, even if they acted in concert with one another. Moreover, these companies are vulnerable to retaliation, including the revocation of their licenses to operate in China. These are not in and of themselves conclusive factors. They do suggest, however, that foreign Internet companies need to carefully consider all potential options for promoting Internet freedom in China in a manner that maximizes effectiveness and minimizes the chance of retaliation. The best way to accomplish both of these goals is to work in concert with, or at least with the support of, other actors. This, in turn, is consistent with another important Fair Share principle: multiple actors owe human rights duties, and the duties of any one actor must be understood in relation to the duties owed by others. Here again the South African apartheid example is instructive. In the case of South Africa, change came through coordinated efforts by many actors. Those companies that stayed in South Africa helped to promote human rights through their actions. However, the most powerful impetus for change came from a series of economic and social sanctions imposed by other nation-states, including exclusion from international sporting events such as the Olympics.[40] One of the most important lessons of the demise of apartheid forms a bedrock principle of the Fair Share theory of corporate responsibility for human rights: multinational corporations cannot be expected to go it alone. Only when the business community acts in concert with national, nongovernmental, and international institutions can it be effective in achieving broad human rights improvements.

Voluntary Guidelines, Trade, and Political Leadership

So how can private corporations, NGOs, and foreign governments best promote Internet freedom in China? The Internet companies have taken a useful first step by beginning to address the censorship issue in concert with one another and with NGOs and the academic community. In late October 2008, Google, Yahoo, and Microsoft, joined by European companies Vodafone and France Telecom, formed the Global Network Initiative—a multi-stakeholder effort including NGOs, such as Human Rights Watch, and academic centers, such as the Berkman Center for Internet and Society at Harvard Law School. The initiative includes an elaborate set of voluntary principles to govern the behavior of Internet companies in countries that restrict Internet freedom.[41] The key components include the promulgation of "Principles on Freedom of Expression and Privacy," "Implementation Guidelines," and a "Governance, Accountability & Learning Framework" to create a vehicle for independent assessment of compliance with the principles and guidelines.[42]

The motivations for establishing the Global Network Initiative are no doubt mixed. It is possible that at least some of these companies experienced a genuine moral awakening and came to realize they have a responsibility to proactively promote Internet freedom. For other companies, it might also be a self-protective response to the intense criticism launched against them by Congress and human rights NGOs. Regardless of the motivation, there are enormous tactical gains to be had by engaging in collective action with other similarly situated companies and in a multi-stakeholder initiative that includes a number of credible NGOs and academics. By working together, the Internet companies minimize the risk of retaliation from governments that engage in censorship. By working with a multi-stakeholder group they can avail themselves of considerable expertise on human rights issues and can also potentially create a formidable group of credible allies that might buffer future criticism.

It will be years before it is possible to fully assess the effectiveness of the Global Network Initiative in combating Internet censorship in China and other countries. Obviously, much will depend on how companies such as Google, MSN, and Yahoo implement the diverse principles and guidelines the initiative has promulgated. From a moral and ethical perspective, the principles and implementation guidelines seem to concede that Internet companies will continue to have "dirty hands" when it comes to Internet censorship in China. Nowhere do the Principles of Freedom of Expression and Privacy suggest that ISPs should not operate in a country that requires them to censor. A number of provisions in the Implementation Guidelines, however, could be potentially significant in assuring that ISPs will meet the standard of "do more good than evil, try to avoid doing a lot of evil, and do no more evil than is necessary" For example, the guidelines provide that:

> When required to restrict communications or remove content, participating companies will...
>
> • interpret government restrictions and demands so as to minimize the negative effect on freedom of expression, and
> • interpret the governmental authority's jurisdiction so as to minimize the negative effect on freedom of expression.

These provisions might logically be read to require precisely the sorts of steps that Google took to limit the number of sites that were censored by its Google.cn search engine. Indeed, the requirement "to minimize the negative effect on freedom of expression" might even be interpreted to require Google to take even bolder steps in their search engine censorship protocol to resist Chinese government censorship.

A second front opened up by the Internet industry in fighting censorship is the WTO. The Internet industry has promoted the idea that Internet censorship constitutes an impermissible barrier to trade, violating the WTO-administered General Agreement on Trade in Services (GATS).[43] This resort to trade dispute mechanisms represents a big collective step for the industry. It is also an unusual step for foreign companies operating in China. As discussed in chapter 5, foreign companies have been sheepish in using any sort of legal process to attempt to resolve disputes with the Chinese government. The fact that the Internet industry is willing to risk offending the Chinese government through a WTO claim may reflect hard business realities. Even though the Internet market has exploded in size in the last decade, collectively, foreign companies have lost significant market share percentage to Chinese companies. For example, in 2002, when the Internet market was at its infancy, Google had a 24 percent share of the search market as compared with Chinese upstart Baidu, which had a mere 3 percent share. By August 2008 Google, which has a dominant share of the U.S. market, had 19 percent of the Chinese search market to Baidu's 65 percent. Business trends do not seem to favor foreign Internet service providers. Making censorship into a WTO dispute may thus signal a sense that foreign companies feel they have less to lose by promoting Internet freedom than they originally thought.

The U.S. government has to date declined to make Internet censorship into a WTO issue. The European Parliament, however, in a 571–38 vote, passed a proposal that, if approved by the European Council, would require the European Union to classify Internet censorship as a barrier to trade. The proposal's sponsor, Jules Maaten of the rightist Dutch VVD (Volkspartij voor Vrijheid en Democratie, or People's Party for Freedom and Democracy), declared that "the 'Great Chinese Firewall' should be seen as an international trade barrier. In addition to American companies like Google, Yahoo, and Microsoft, European Internet companies like Wanadoo, Telecom Italia, and France Telecom have to unwillingly censor their services in authoritarian states."[44]

On a different legal theory, the European Union, the United States, and Canada filed a WTO complaint that China's requirement that foreign financial news services affiliate with the state-owned Xinhua violates China's GATS commitment to treat foreign companies no less favorably than domestic companies. In November 2008, this action was settled. China agreed to establish an independent regulator and licensing authority. Bloomberg L.P. said the agreement allowed it to "establish a robust commercial presence for our financial information services in China."[45]

Time will tell whether the tactic of confronting China through the WTO will prove to be an effective way to promote Internet freedom in China. History suggests that the threat of economic sanctions—especially when not part of a coordinated and comprehensive human rights foreign policy—is not an effective way to pressure China. Prior to China's accession to the WTO, the United States unsuccessfully threatened economic sanctions against China to protest human rights conditions. One important reason for the failure of sanctions was that, unlike South Africa, which was a relatively minor economic power, China has enormous economic leverage. As a result, the attempt to pressure China simply didn't work.[46] Moreover, China has become even more powerful economically since the failed Clinton initiative. At the same time, however, through its WTO membership, China has become more deeply enmeshed in the international trading system, legal rules, and institutions.

The European Parliament's willingness to treat Internet censorship as a trade issue provides an interesting contrast with the U.S. Congress, which put on a big show by requiring Internet executives to testify and then proceeded to harangue and embarrass them. The conspicuous display of indignation was not matched, as it was in Europe, with any concrete actions. Indeed, the one piece of legislation introduced in Congress took a very different approach from the European legislation and was never even close to coming up for a vote. Instead of making Internet censorship into a trade issue, H.R. 275, the Global Online Freedom Act, proposed to punish Internet providers by subjecting them to financial liability for engaging in certain acts of censorship on foreign soil.[47]

The contrast between the actions of the European Parliament and the grandstanding of the U.S. Congress merely highlights the general lack of leadership and decisive action from either the U.S. Congress or the executive branch on human rights in China. Activists outside and inside China have certainly done their fair share to document, publicize, and create accountability for government and private-sector Internet censorship, often at great personal risk. However, until the U.S. government joins Europe in taking tangible and public steps to promote Internet freedom, it is simply not realistic to expect Western Internet companies to have much success—even when acting collectively and through multi-stakeholder initiatives—in promoting Internet freedom in China.

At the end of the day, it is unlikely that Internet censorship in China will end simply because it technically violates the terms of the GATS. This is not to say that a trade claim should not be pursued, but the real battle is one of ideas not legal maneuvers. Ultimately, Westerners can have the biggest impact by making a clear and forceful case for the place of freedom in a modern, developed society. The Global Network Initiative principles can only be effectively implemented with active support of the U.S. government. Much will depend on the role human rights will play in the foreign policy of the Obama Presidency. Unless President Obama and other administration officials such as Secretary of State Hillary Clinton speak out on human rights in China, the actions of NGOs and Internet companies will have little impact.

As we have seen in this chapter, the Internet will be the focal point within China in the next decade for a great national debate and struggle about free speech rights. Western nations can and should have a voice in this debate. Thus far in the twenty-first century, however, U.S. foreign policy has been conspicuously muted in its criticisms of human rights conditions in China. The contrast between the two most recent U.S. presidents is instructive. When President Bill Clinton traveled to China in June 1988 he gave a forceful speech at Beijing University (Beida) in which he called for improvements in human rights conditions in no uncertain terms. Quoting Benjamin Franklin, Clinton said that "our critics are our friends, for they show us our faults." Clinton actively engaged the students at Beida in a wide-ranging dialogue about human rights. It was a powerful moment that was televised throughout China.[48] By contrast, when President Bush traveled to China in November 2005, he gave his major statement about human rights in China while he was in Japan, before arriving in China.[49] Once in China he limited his dialogue on human rights to "quiet diplomacy" and emphasized only the rights of Christians to practice religion freely, an issue that played more to his evangelical constituency in the United States than to Chinese citizens.[50]

By the time President Bush returned to China for the 2008 Olympics, human rights issues had completely fallen off his radar. U.S. foreign policy had fallen into lock step with the business community's desire to avoid jeopardizing its perceived economic interests. Looking to the future, one can only hope that President Obama and Secretary Clinton will have the vision, courage, and will to engage China in a meaningful dialogue about Internet freedom and other human rights issues. If the U.S. President and the Congress are unwilling or incapable of effectively promoting human rights in the context of a broad-ranging and complicated relationship with China, then Western Internet companies, as they struggle with the difficult task of reconciling their human rights duties with their duties to shareholders, have little chance of effecting any meaningful change in China— through voluntary guidelines or through WTO legal claims.

5

Soft Seat* on the Long March

Foreign Business and the Rule of Law in China

One of the most far-reaching and crucial aspects of China's social and political transformation in the coming decade will be the growing importance of law and impersonal, neutrally applied rules. A fair and independent judicial system is essential to the emergence of human rights and democratic government. The path of this transformation is, however, far from secure.

The coming decade will witness a struggle between the rule of law and the persistent vestiges of the clientalist state. Corruption and a culture of securing economic goods by cultivating good relationships with authoritarian government officials will continue to play an important role in political and economic life. Powerful political and economic forces have vested interests in slowing down the emergence of a rule of law. It is in the context of this struggle that this chapter will consider the impact and

---

* In the Chinese rail system, "soft seat" (*ruanzuo*) is first class with amenities such as air conditioning, padded chairs, and Western-style toilets.

moral responsibilities of foreign firms. Although the role of foreigners is modest in relation to indigenous forces, foreign companies have an opportunity and indeed a moral duty to contribute to the development of the rule of law in China.

In the coming decade, economic reform will wholly dismantle the "iron rice bowl," one of the key institutional pillars of the Communist era. As the government becomes less involved as an owner and operator of the economy, ordinary Chinese citizens will no longer have to rely on good personal relations with government officials for access to economic and social goods. The "iron rice bowl" symbolized the idea that the socialist state guaranteed lifetime employment, housing, medical benefits, retirement income, and education for all citizens.[1] But this guarantee came with a huge price and was in its own way fraught with uncertainty. The *gongzuo danwei* or work unit was the Communist Party's principal method of control. It was through the work unit that the government compiled secret dossiers or *danan* to detect potential dissidents. Any perceived political deviance would be met with a salary cut, a housing reassignment, or the like. The system was highly personalized and arbitrary. Every citizen's access to social goods was heavily dependent on good relations with the immediate work unit supervisor and there was little effective right of appeal when injustice occurred.[2]

A poignant moment in Da Chen's remarkable memoir of coming of age in China at the dawn of economic reform comes when Chen's father, whose own life had been ruined because he was part of the politically incorrect landlord class, realizes that his sons will be able to attend college. "Mao has gone west and now you have a chance to try," Chen's father says.[3] He means to suggest that after Mao's death, China, under Deng Xiaoping, had adopted Western free-market principles of merit-based access to social and economic goods such as college. Da Chen's generation and those that have come afterward already enjoy a freedom to pursue their dreams that was unimaginable under the clientalist, political correctness regime that dominated access to economic and social goods in the pre-reform era.

In marked contrast with the arbitrariness and culture of personal relationships or *guanxi* predominating in the Communist era, in the post-reform era Chinese citizens are acquiring economic goods and social status through hard work and merit.[4] In the coming decade, this emerging meritocracy will increasingly rely on impartial administrative rules and legally enforceable rights to protect and secure its economic and social gains. This idea—that economic and social goods can be protected as a legal right by an independent judicial system against encroachment by the government—is a radical notion in China.

As with virtually all of the dramatic changes that will occur in the next decade, the principal forces and motivations that will determine how securely China embraces notions of procedural justice and the rule of law are internally driven and reflect distinctively Chinese preoccupations and perspectives. Nevertheless, foreign companies can and should play a crucial role. To date, foreigners have had a mixed record. On the positive side, foreign companies have been at the forefront of the struggle for greater legal transparency. However, Western companies have demonstrated a conspicuous lack of moral courage in challenging government actions through the judicial system. They have relied instead on what they regard as the safer and smarter course of cultivating good relations with government officials. Thus, at the very time that progressive forces in China are struggling to break through the clientalist system and establish a fair and independent rule of law, foreign firms are lending support and legitimacy to the old regime. Randall Peerenboom compared the slow development of the rule of law in China to Mao's "Long March."[5] Foreign companies have so far been content to take the "soft seat" in this difficult journey.

Rule of Law or Rule by Law?

Legal experts tell two very different stories about the current role and status of law in Chinese society. To hear one side (let's call this the Constitutionalist view), there is no rule of law in China. Unlike the constitutions of the United Kingdom, the United States, and other countries with well-established legal systems, the legislative, administrative, and judicial powers are not separated. The Supreme Judicial Court and the entire judicial branch have no independent power to interpret the meaning of Chinese law. Quite the contrary—judicial decisions are subject to the heavy-handed control of the Chinese Communist Party. Because of this lack of judicial independence, the Constitutionalists believe, it is nonsensical to speak of a true rule "of law" as much as a rule "by law." Law does not function as a check on government power and abuse. It serves instead as an instrument of government control over ordinary citizens.

Other legal experts (let's call them the Legitimists) tell a very different story of a China in which law is becoming an important part of the daily lives of ordinary citizens. Indeed, in the first decade of the twenty-first century, the Chinese government passed a long list of new or revised laws governing, among other things, labor relations, contracts, intellectual property, antitrust, insurance, and corporate and securities regulation. Moreover, millions of Chinese citizens are turning to courts, administrative tribunals, and arbitrators to resolve disputes among themselves and even disputes with the government. According to the Legitimists, law is one of the fastest-growing and most important phenomena in contemporary China. It is serving a role in peacefully channeling social conflict and discontent.[6]

In his seminal book on the subject, Stanley B. Lubman compared the place of law in China to a "bird in a cage."[7] As the phrase implies, various factors prevent the emergence of the rule of law in China. One major constraint is the lack of educational qualifications, professionalism, and competency of the lawyers and judges. Other factors are institutional such as the fact that in China the courts are treated as agencies on a par with other agencies of government and the fact that judges show great deference to the decisions of other government agencies. Also hindering the formation of an impartial and independent judiciary are corruption (further fed by the poor pay among judges) and local protectionism (exacerbated by the appointment and pay of local judges by local legislatures). As a result of such factors, courts tend to favor local companies in commercial disputes and local officials in cases brought by ordinary citizens.[8]

Perhaps the most significant factor constraining the development of the rule of law is a fundamentally political one—that is, the constitutionally enshrined dominance of the Chinese Communist Party (CCP) over the Chinese state and government. The President of the Supreme People's Court ranks well below the minister of Public Security in the CCP hierarchy, in a pattern mirrored at the local level. The influence and control of the CCP over virtually every agency of the government is difficult to overstate.[9] The institutional status of the judiciary in China is no greater or more immune from political influence than that of any other government agency. The magnitude of this influence can be appreciated from simply walking around a typical courthouse where Party officials unabashedly work out of offices with conspicuous signs announcing their presence.

One area in which China has made significant progress is in the education and professionalism of its judges and lawyers. More than 50 percent of the judges in China hold a law degree, compared to less than 7 percent in 1995. There are more than six thousand law professors and 150,000 lawyers. Tens of thousands of lawyers pass the bar exam each year and many of the finest of them are going to work as judges and arbitrators. This represents enormous progress for the rule of law from the beginning of the reform period when there were three thousand lawyers in all of China. Thanks to programs such as those sponsored by the Ford Foundation, the American Bar Association, and the Europe-China Academic Network, Chinese lawyers and judges are gaining broad exposure to their counterparts from other nations. This increasing professionalism and exposure to foreign lawyers in turn is leading the courts to assume a bolder and more independent role. Columbia Law School professor Benjamin L. Liebman reports that judges are "increasingly looking to other courts and judges, rather than party superiors, in deciding novel or difficult cases. As a result, courts are increasingly coming into conflict with other state institutions, [and] growing numbers of well-educated judges are developing professional identities."[10] In July 2002, Xiao Yang, then president of the Supreme People's Court, made a strong case for reducing political interference in judicial affairs, falling just short of calling outright for judicial independence: "Courts have often been taken as branches of the government, and judges viewed as civil servants who have to follow orders from superiors, which prevents them from exercising mandated legal duties."[11]

The ultimate path to a true rule of law will require dramatic political transformation. In the coming decade, the emergence of an independent judiciary hinges on whether the Communist Party will, as New York University law professor Jerome Cohen has stated, "surrender its power to dictate decisions in individual court cases and place the party and government under the law, not above it." Cohen envisions the emergence of a leader at the highest levels of the Communist Party with the sophistication and persuasive abilities to press for legal reform in the same way that an earlier generation pressed for economic reform. He places great hope in the promotion of Li Keqiang, a relatively young leader trained in law at Beijing University, to the nine-member Politburo Standing Committee.[12] Time will tell whether such a profound change will occur at the highest levels of the Chinese government.

Despite hopeful signs, it is far from inevitable that the coming decade will herald the emergence of an independent judiciary and true rule of law. Indeed, recent developments strongly suggest that the government is intent on increasing its control over the courts. In June 2008, Wang Shengjun, newly promoted to president of the Supreme People's Court, told court officials to "unify our consciousness, thoughts and action regarding what kind of flag the courts will hoist and what road to take…in order to ensure the correct political direction of the people's courts." According to long-time China political observer Willy Lam, Wang's statement results from a concerted high-level effort led by Chinese president Hu Jintao to bring the judiciary under the control of the party-state. Hu declared in June 2008 that the foremost task of the judiciary should be to "steadfastly safeguard the CCP's ruling party status, as well as national security and the people's interest."[13]

If somehow the political space in the Chinese political structure can be created, China's Supreme People's Court must also evolve to a point of public support and prestige where it will feel empowered to seize the moment for itself and assert its judicial authority to interpret the law. China's judicial system needs, as it were, a *Marbury v. Madison* moment. In that case, decided in 1803, the U.S. Supreme Court asserted the court's independent power to review the constitutionality of statutes and the legality of administrative actions. In the first decade of the twenty-first century China's Supreme People's Court does not possess the institutional power or sociopolitical legitimacy to make a similar ruling. However, even within a repressive Asian regime, it is not quixotic to suggest that the next decade could possibly bring such a *Marbury v. Madison* moment. In July 2007, for example, the Indonesian Constitutional Court asserted its own judicial independence when it declared unconstitutional "hate sowing" offenses—left over from the Dutch colonial administration—that criminalized "public expression of feelings of hostility, hatred or contempt toward the government."[14]

Despite evident flaws of the judicial system, the past decade has witnessed a veritable explosion of laws and legal institutions. Some observers maintain that these legal developments have served a useful conflict-management role:

> Today we are witnessing an outpouring of grievances from, among others, people who lost money in the stock market, pensioners, veterans, unemployed laborers, disgruntled peasants, and unhappy couples. Yet, only a small proportion of these complaints spread to other sectors, lead to violence, or threaten the existence of the regime. Institutions like courts, arbitration commissions, and mediators have all played a notable role in channeling social discontent into moderated forums.[15]

In the coming decade, many ordinary citizens will continue to utilize the legal system, flawed as it is, to slowly chip away at the authoritarian power of the government. "This is the way dripping water wears through a rock," legal activist Hao Jinsong has said. "People...have to land successive blows on an unfair system before it collapses." Hao is one of a new breed of activists in the nascent *weiquan* (rights defense) movement. These lawyers use the courts to challenge the actions of the government. Hao is a kind of folk hero in China for bringing a series of lawsuits that eventually compelled the Ministry of Railways to issue receipts for items purchased aboard a train. The result was an increase in the taxes paid by the national railroad. "Every time I sit in a court across from the defendant of a government ministry and argue ferociously for the public interest," Hao says, "I am already a winner."[16]

After his daughter suffered brain damage and paralysis from what was supposed to be a routine vaccination, Liang Yongli pressed on for years until a court finally agreed to hear a case against a state-owned drug company and against provincial and city health officials in his native Guangdong. For an ordinary citizen like Liang, taking on the government through litigation requires great bravery. Another father, whose daughter suffered similar symptoms, dropped out of the litigation because he feared government reprisal. "I can't sleep," he wrote Liang in a text message. "I thought about it all night. They are too powerful."[17]

Although many Chinese citizens have taken to civil litigation and arbitration with gusto, this trend is unlikely to continue in the coming decade unless courts continue to become more professional and independent. Minxin Pei of the Carnegie Endowment for International Peace has observed that after peaking in 1999 civil and commercial litigation declined by 12 percent over a three-year period. Pei believes that this decline was due to the fact that in roughly the same period the success rate of plaintiffs suing the government declined from 41 percent to under 21 percent. Pei thinks it likely that "the decreasing probability of receiving judicial relief through the administrative litigation process has discouraged many citizens from taking their cases to the courts."[18] Instead, millions of Chinese citizens have pursued claims against the government through the less adversarial, Communist-era *xinfang* (letters and visits) system of directly petitioning government offices.[19]

Pei's research underscores both the promise and peril of legal reform in the coming decade. Will China develop a legitimate, professional judiciary that will permit ordinary citizens to challenge government actions in court? The answer to this question is far from certain. Moreover, Westerners potentially have a crucial role to play in this process. The emergence of the rule of law in the coming decade will partly depend on whether foreign corporations and lawyers possess the moral courage to do their fair share to foster the development of the rule of law. Before we turn to understanding the role of foreigners in this process, however, it is worthwhile to consider how, as a result of China's accession into the WTO, the legal rights of foreign corporations and the legal rights of ordinary citizens have become inextricably intertwined.

The WTO and China's Court System

Ironically, what is perhaps the most important advance for the rule of law in the reform era, the Administrative Litigation Law (ALL),[20] was promulgated on April 4, 1989, virtually the very day that pro-democracy protesters began to occupy Tiananmen Square. The ALL empowers individuals to sue public agencies and officials, an unprecedented possibility in Chinese history. To be sure there are limitations to the ALL when compared to the remedies available under administrative law in countries with a fully developed rule of law. Most significantly, ALL plaintiffs may only challenge specific, concrete acts, such as the withholding of a license. The purpose of the ALL is to ensure that administrative agencies make their decisions in accordance with the law. Courts may not question the appropriateness or reasonableness of an administrative agency's decision. Nor may plaintiffs challenge the rule-making authority of an agency over a particular subject matter. China does not have an administrative procedures law that would specify the procedures and standards that administrative agencies must adhere to when promulgating rules and regulations. Although legal experts have been drafting one over a number of years, it is unclear when China will be ready for independent judicial review of the legality of administrative rule making.[21]

The legal institutions created under the ALL for ordinary Chinese citizens coincidentally are the very same ones that China has designated to comply with its legal reform obligations under the WTO. Hence in the ALL one finds an unusual confluence of foreign-investment driven and domestically driven institutional change. Shockingly, however, in almost a decade since China's accession to the WTO, not even one foreign business has ever exercised the rights guaranteed under the WTO! Before discussing the reasons behind this failure by foreign companies to utilize the legal system in disputes with the government, it is worth understanding the legal reform obligations that were created when China joined the WTO.

After a nation applies to join the WTO, a "working party" of members is formed and series of multilateral and bilateral negotiations are held. Once two-thirds of the WTO members vote in favor of the accession, the applicant is permitted to join, subject to its working party commitments. The final terms of China's accession to the WTO in 2001 are contained in three documents: the Working Party Report, the Accession Protocol, and schedules containing specific commitments in particular economic sectors.[22] The substantive legal requirements arising from China's WTO accession are similar to those applicable to other nations. This is in contrast to China's other commitments, most notably in the services sector, where China went considerably beyond what had been required of other nations joining the WTO.[23]

Three provisions in the underlying trade agreements oblige China—as they would any other WTO member—to reform its legal system. Article X(3)(a) of the General Agreement on Tariffs and Trade (GATT) requires members to "maintain, or institute as soon as practicable, judicial, arbitral or administrative tribunals or procedures for the purpose, *inter alia,* of the prompt review and correction of administrative action relating to customs matters. Such tribunals or procedures shall be independent of the agencies entrusted with administrative enforcement."[24] Part V of the Trade-Related Aspects of Intellectual Property Rights (TRIPS) agreement requires a dispute resolution system for intellectual property rights.[25] Finally, Article VI(2)(a) of the General Agreement on Trade in Services (GATS) requires WTO members to "maintain or institute as soon as practicable judicial, arbitral or administrative tribunals or procedures which provide, at the request of an affected service supplier, for the prompt review of, and where justified, appropriate remedies for, administrative decisions affecting trade in services."[26]

In the Accession Protocol, China committed to three specific areas of legal reform—increased transparency, uniform application of the law, and judicial review of administrative rulings. In the area of transparency, China agreed not to enforce unpublished laws and to "make available...upon request, all laws, regulations, and other measures pertaining to or affecting trade...before such measures are implemented and enforced."[27] This idea that laws and regulations would be open to prior comment from those affected is a novel one in Chinese legal history. China also agreed to "administer in a uniform, impartial and uniform manner all its laws, regulations, rules, decrees, directives, administrative guidance, policies and other measures...pertaining to or affecting trade in goods, services, trade-related aspects of intellectual property rights or the control of foreign exchange."[28] The most significant undertaking in China's WTO accession was a commitment to independent judicial review of administrative action. The Accession Protocol clearly set forth this unprecedented, indeed revolutionary, requirement of independent judicial review: "China shall establish or designate and maintain tribunals, contact points and procedures for the prompt review of all disputes relating to the implementation of laws, regulations, judicial decisions and administrative rulings of general application....Such tribunals shall be impartial and independent of the agencies entrusted with administrative enforcement."[29]

The Accession Protocol raised a number of interesting questions about the future of the rule of law in China. How would China implement its WTO legal reform requirements? Would it create a separate law and court system for WTO issues? Or would it adjudicate foreign claims in the already existing court system? In August 2002, China's Supreme People's Court addressed some of these questions by issuing an edict that the WTO claims of foreigners would be based on the ALL and would be tried in a special section of the administrative division of intermediate courts.[30] In short, foreigners must use the same laws and the same courts as ordinary Chinese citizens to press their claims against the Chinese government.

Because foreign corporations are using the same legal system as ordinary citizens, the participation of foreign companies and lawyers in civil litigation against the government can have a profound effect on the emergence of the rule of law in the coming decade. Will foreign companies exercise the legal rights granted to them by the WTO and demand independent judicial review of arbitrary or illegal government actions? Or will foreigners seek to resolve such disputes by traditional means such as *guanxi* or perhaps even through outright bribery? To date, the results have been stunningly disappointing. In a series of confidential interviews conducted in China in May 2006 and October 2007, no attorney representing foreign interests in China was aware of *any* instance in which a foreign company attempted to use the ALL to resolve a dispute with any Chinese governmental authority.[31]

To be sure, foreign companies do contribute to development of the rule of law by using the civil court system to resolve disputes with other companies, both domestic and foreign. For example, in a high-profile ruling in June 2006, Pfizer won an important victory in Beijing's No. 1 Intermediate People's Court preventing twelve Chinese companies from manufacturing generic versions of the erectile dysfunction drug Viagra.[32] Although Pfizer won its intellectual property dispute in a civil court proceeding, in his research political scientist Andrew C. Mertha observed broadly among foreign firms a "shift from civil litigation to administrative enforcement to criminal prosecution."[33] It is one thing, however, to sue another company or to cajole the Chinese government to use its police power to control and punish intellectual property violations. It is quite another thing entirely for companies to summon up the courage to sue the Chinese government itself.

"Treading Carefully": Perspectives of Lawyers Representing Foreign Companies

Among the attorneys interviewed there was a wide range of opinions about the likelihood, timing, and even in some cases the desirability of the emergence of a fair trial system and a strong system of judicial review. One partner who had practiced business law for a prestigious global law firm described how the inability to access an independent judiciary affected the way he practiced law in China as compared with other areas of the world:

> Representing business interests in China is very different from any other area of the world, even other developing countries. In countries like Brazil, Mexico, and even in India there are very clear avenues of appeal. Often, when practicing in those countries you would try to get a clear negative ruling from a government official because, once the agency acted formally, you knew that you could appeal the ruling up the governmental chain and if necessary though the court system. But in China it is often difficult to tell who is in charge and there is no possibility of an independent judicial review.

Therefore, this lawyer cautions, in words that sadly capture the spirit of the foreign legal and business community in Beijing, "one must tread carefully."[34]

A Chinese-born and U.S.-trained attorney working for a Fortune 500 company believes that the time has come for the courts to play a role in the resolution of disputes between business interests and the state. He optimistically predicts it will happen within five years. "In the past," he notes, "the resolution of such disputes often took place through good connections or nonpublic negotiations. But the possibility of bringing a case before an independent judge will change that dynamic."[35] Another attorney who has studied the court systems in both the United States and China believes that change will come slowly and will depend less on the initiative of the foreign business community and more on the will of China's rulers. He observes that "what is really possible is very limited....Only when the Chinese Communist Party wants to send the signal that the system should change will the system actually change. Until the CCP allows change, change will not happen in the legal system."[36]

Another highly experienced lawyer, born and trained in China and working for a U.S.-based Fortune 500 company, has a very different perspective. She views the emergence of a U.S.-style adversarial legal environment in China with great circumspection. She cautions that "the establishment of the rule of law in China is a long process. Fighting in court is only one way that a rule of law can emerge." She questions whether the use of litigation is a "socially responsible way to resolve a dispute when it can be resolved through discussion, conciliation, and a process of mutual education."[37]

The foreign business community has chosen not to exercise its legal rights under the WTO even though U.S. and European trade negotiators went through a lot of trouble to establish these legal rights. What can explain the sheepish behavior of foreign companies? Multinational corporations regularly challenge government actions in court not only in the United States and Europe but also in developing countries such as Mexico, Brazil, and India. The behavior of foreign companies in China, where "treading carefully" continues to be the mantra for lawyers and businesspersons alike, is truly exceptional. The foreign business community calculates that challenging any unit, national, provincial, or local, of the Chinese party-state is not in their commercial self-interest. Lawyers and businesspeople interviewed about the subject offer two basic reasons for their caution in challenging government actions through the judicial system. First, they have little confidence in the fairness of the system. Because of the enormous systemic problems with the independence and professionalism of the judiciary outlined above, foreign businesspeople and lawyers simply do not believe they can get a fair and full hearing of their claims in court. Second, they are afraid of retaliation. Even taking into account that sometimes litigation is not always the most productive way to resolve disputes, the fact that this path has *never* been taken in China leaves one with an inescapable and sobering conclusion: foreign companies and lawyers are afraid to stand up for their legal rights. They are afraid that government will retaliate against their business interests if they challenge their rulings in court.

One prominent foreign lawyer who has practiced for decades in Shanghai sounds the conventional wisdom and worldview of the typical Westerner practicing law in China. (Technically, foreign lawyers cannot practice law in China but they are able to do so by affiliating with local attorneys.) He believes that "it would be naïve in the extreme to believe that a right on paper could be effectively enforced in a PRC administrative court against a government agency." He says that "in my experience I never saw any of my clients attempting to sue a government agency. They recognized that their chances of success—their chance even of getting the courts to accept a case like that—were almost zero." As do other lawyers practicing in China, he advocates nonconfrontational resolution of disputes with government agencies.[38]

Of course, as this prominent Shanghai lawyer notes, "in the U.S. you might do the same thing with a government agency because you don't want to antagonize them either." There is, however, a very big difference between negotiating with a Chinese government official and negotiating with a U.S. government official. If negotiations with a U.S. official don't work and the stakes are high enough, corporations will challenge government actions in the courts. "In the U.S. people are not afraid of litigation because there is at least the sense that while litigation may be a crap shoot, the judge is generally impartial," observes the lawyer, "but you don't get that sense in China." He insists that it is "incredibly naïve" to suggest that foreign companies should sue the Chinese government in the case of disputes:

> Business is already at a disadvantage in China because of a bias in favor of Chinese companies. Also, you have to deal on a regular basis with the lever of power and the levers of the abuse of power in those agencies. If you want to pull your business out of China, then fine, sue a government agency. If you want to stay and operate there and you do not want people who are sabotaging you, then you will think twice about suing a government agency. The failure to enforce a theoretical right is not a failure in some moral duty. It is a prudent and sensible assessment of the consequences of availing yourself of what is really a phantom right.

Instead of securing their economic interests through legal rights as they do virtually everywhere else in the world, the typical Western executive and her lawyer have come to rely exclusively on cultivating relationships or *guanxi,* particularly with powerful public figures. "If you have *guanxi,*" claims one Western business executive, "there is little you can't accomplish.... There are few rules in China that can't be broken or at least bent, by people or firms with the right *guanxi.*"[39] Westerners have taken to the idea of *guanxi* with gusto. In doing so, many Westerners believe they are acting in a culturally sensitive manner and penetrating deeply into layers of Chinese civilization. Never mind that *guanxi* can come and go with the people you are cultivating or that someone else may come along and upset your plans by having even better *guanxi* than you. Never mind also that within Chinese culture true *guanxi* has very subtle social origins, limits, and is based on some element of true personal affection or *ganqing*.[40] For many Western executives in contemporary China, *guanxi* has in practice become a simple economic exchange, a practical means of achieving quid pro quo. Sometimes the attempt to establish *guanxi* with high Chinese officials is luridly bereft of principle, as in the case of Rupert Murdoch, who, when seeking to make an investment in China, denounced the Dalai Lama by favorably quoting someone who called him "a very old political monk shuffling around in Gucci shoes." Murdoch also cancelled the book contract of former Hong Kong Governor Chris Patten because he was afraid the book might offend the Chinese government. "We are trying to set up in China," Murdoch said at the time. "Why should we upset them? Let somebody else upset them."[41] In its worst manifestation, Westerners practice a perverse interpretation of *guanxi* that is simply a euphemism for out and out corruption and bribery as more subtle social rituals are replaced by the coarse exchange of money for favors.[42]

Foreign Business and Commercial Bribery

One of the more disappointing developments in the post-Tiananmen era has been the shameful manner that many so-called world-class companies have embraced shady business practices. To be sure, corruption and bribery are so endemic in China that it is extremely difficult to do business there honestly. This is particularly true for smaller firms that may not have financial resources or marketplace power to succeed without paying bribes. James McGregor, the former China bureau chief for the *Wall Street Journal,* has observed that "once you get below the level of big multinationals doing large deals, China becomes a swamp."[43] What is especially disappointing, however, is that even supposedly world-class multinational companies with great financial resources are willing to risk their global reputations to make a quick buck in China.

Official corruption statistics paint a sordid picture. In Transparency International's Corruption Perception Index for 2006, China scores 3.3 (up from 3.2 in 2005) on a scale of 1 (most corrupt) to 10. China was ranked 70th (an improvement from 78th) of 160 countries surveyed. In 2004 almost three thousand officials at or above the county level were investigated.

The Communist Party's own internal investigations unit has punished over 170,000 party members for corruption. Just in the first half of 2005, over sixteen hundred employees of financial institutions were punished for corruption.[44] Official government statistics only tell part of the story. The vast bulk of bribery and corruption goes undetected and unpunished. As great wealth is being created in China the temptation to skim a little bit off the top is irresistible for many government officers, Party officials, their friends, and family members. The corruption runs so deep that, despite various showy anticorruption campaigns, one has to question whether there is really the will to root out corruption in the CCP and the government.

If you bring up the subject with any businessperson, foreign or domestic, from big company or small, the reaction will uniformly be one of resignation over the overwhelming pervasiveness of bribes and kickbacks both in private business transactions and in dealings with the government. The *Economist* observed that corruption has gotten so bad that foreign executives claim to be "overwhelmed by the business of kickbacks."[45] However, the sobering truth is that some foreign firms seem to be as much perpetrators as victims of corruption. As economic analyst and China watcher Daniel Rosen has observed, foreign executives "contribute to the cloud of corruption often observed to hang over China's commercial environment."[46]

The corrupt practices of supposedly "world-class" multinationals have attracted the attention of the Chinese government, media, and public. In November 2006, the No. 1 Intermediate Court in Beijing sentenced Zhang Enzhao, the former head of China Construction Bank, to fifteen years in prison for accepting more than $500,000 in bribes. The court's verdict noted that two American companies, IBM and NCR, indirectly paid bribes to Zhang to win information technology services contracts with the bank. According to the court, the two companies paid "service fees" to a "consultant," Zou Jianhua, who in turn paid bribes to Zhang, including a pair of Tiffany watches and a luxury apartment in Shanghai worth over $300,000. Both companies have denied knowledge of any bribery, but the court's ruling was based on the testimony of former company officials.[47]

IBM and NCR are hardly isolated cases. In April 2004, Lucent Technologies announced that it had fired four executives, including the president, chief operating officer, and finance manager of its China operations, for potential violations of the United States Foreign Corrupt Practices Act (FCPA), which makes it illegal for American companies or their agents to pay bribes to foreign officials.[48] In May 2005, Diagnostic Products Corp. pled guilty to violating the FCPA by paying bribes to doctors who worked in public hospitals in China.[49] These high-profile incidents have tarnished the reputation of all multinationals. A Chinese-born and U.S.-trained attorney working for a Fortune 500 company observed that "many Chinese have begun to ask why foreign corporations paid such bribes in China, but not in their home countries."[50]

After Diagnostic Products pled guilty in the United States, Professor Cheng Baoku, who heads the Research Institute of International Economic Law at the Tianjin-based Nankai University, published a series of studies that caught the attention of the highest levels of the Chinese government. Cheng did not pull any punches in questioning the government's own failure of oversight and even complicity. "This case damaged the image of the Chinese market," Cheng wrote, "but why didn't the Chinese government discover it? Why were the Chinese medical staff and hospitals involved protected by local authorities?" Cheng also meted out considerable blame for foreign business executives: "It is easier for overseas firms to rake in huge profits in China if they bend themselves to those underlying rules. Severer punishments of foreign companies are needed.... The government has the responsibility to expose and punish all commercial bribery cases.... Afterward, other companies will not trust the companies involved in those cases. In this way, the motive of offering bribes will be eliminated."[51]

Cheng found that commercial bribery was so common that many companies believed that the practice of bribery was a "tactical rule" of the Chinese market, especially in the medical, pharmaceutical, construction, and technology industries. The Diagnostic Products scandal is just the "tip of the iceberg," Cheng observed. "In the past, people took commercial bribery as a means of marketing from the perspective of competition laws. However, it has become one of the factors that is causing corruption and the instability of Chinese economy and politics." Cheng urged the establishment of a uniform Anti-Unfair Competition Law of the People's Republic of China and also suggested improvements in accounting systems.[52]

Cheng's articles drew the attention of the Central Committee of the CCP and the central government, including Chinese president Hu Jintao.[53]

Other observers, such as Dan Wei of the Supreme People's Procuratorate of the People's Republic of China, believe that China's underdeveloped financial system and the fragmented power among government agencies are also major barriers to suppressing commercial bribery. "Companies are in a disadvantageous position in China. They need to grow. It is hard for them to stay away from briberies if other companies are benefiting from conducting briberies. It is a problem of the whole system," commented Dan on a television show highlighting commercial-bribery.[54]

Western companies that pay bribes undermine the most fundamental moral premises of economic engagement in China—the idea that Western businesses are contributing to greater economic, personal, and political freedom in China. The market economy is in very far-reaching ways breaking down personalized, *guanxi*-based power relations in China. As Doug Guthrie has observed, "industrial managers no longer need to curry favor with state officials to overcome bottlenecks or gain access to resources, and, as a result, they do not view *guanxi* practice as an important part of decision-making in China's industrial economy."[55] When Chinese business executives and ordinary Chinese citizens observe supposedly world-class Western businesses paying bribes it profoundly undermines this putative transformation. It is not just the companies paying the bribes that lose their moral authority. The reputations of all multinationals are tarnished. A study by Chinese researchers found that "more than half of commercial bribery in China in the past decade involved foreign businessmen."[56] A Xinhua Economic Information Service Report offered a scathing indictment of foreign companies: "Corruption is widespread in Chinese business and the multinationals that swarmed into the Chinese market to seek their fortune when the country opened its doors must bear part of the blame. Multinationals were hailed for introducing concepts of market-driven competition and business fair play, and for bringing in capital, but it seems that many of them have adapted to the local business environment in the wrong way."[57]

The tendency of foreign companies to associate themselves with "middlemen" who pay bribes constitutes the flip side of the coin of their reluctance to protect their legal rights through the judicial system. They both display a preference to conduct business in China according to the old rules of good connections. As we have seen, many individuals in China are embracing change and attempting, often bravely, to assert their legal rights in court. Yet the foreign business community has opted to secure its economic interests exclusively through friendly, sometimes corrupt, relations with government and party officials.

Foreign Business and Legal Transparency: Planting the Seedbed for the New Labor Contract Law

One area in which foreign companies, and in particular foreign law firms, have made a significant contribution to the development of the rule of law is in transparency. This is a classic instance of "doing good" for China by "doing well" and pursuing their self-interest. Businesses are reluctant to invest capital and make operational plans without predictable and secure property rights. A cornerstone of such economic rights is legal transparency. On the most basic level legal transparency was sorely lacking in China two decades into the reform era. Important commercial laws and regulations were sometimes not even published and made available to the public. Lawyers representing foreign companies would sometimes find out about a pertinent statute or regulation only in private meetings with government officials. The Chinese government most certainly was not in the habit of consulting with interested parties *before* a law or regulation was passed.

One U.S.-trained partner in an international law firm who has practiced law in China for almost two decades notes that "the foreign business community has had a significant impact on transparency. This has been a critical issue for business. As a result, the Ministry of Commerce now publishes a weekly gazette of its regulations." In addition to transparency, he notes, "the foreign business community has had an unprecedented input into the drafting of laws. The Contract Law, Antitrust Law, Labor Contract Law, and other proposed laws have all been drafted with significant input from the business community."[58]

Prior input into the drafting of commercial laws by the business community has had a significant spillover effect on the general population and the rule of law. This influence was dramatically in evidence in the passage of the new Labor Contract Law by the Standing Committee of the National People's Congress. The process by which the law was passed is in many ways as groundbreaking as its substance. The worker protections incorporated in the law were the direct result of Western-style lobbying by an indigenous labor rights movement in China. "When the Labor Contract Law was being drafted," notes one lawyer, "the business community was unhappy with some its provisions and it made its views known to the government."[59]

Never before had the government solicited and received such extensive input over many months from the workers and companies that would be affected by the law. A few months after the first draft was circulated in 2004, Chinese leaders took the unprecedented step of seeking public comment. The response was extraordinary. The government reported nearly two hundred thousand comments. Some came from large companies such as General Electric and Microsoft and umbrella trade organizations such as the American Chamber of Commerce. However, the overwhelming majority came from ordinary workers organized in a campaign by the ACFTU. Numerous advocates for labor, both within and outside China, were highly critical of the attempts by the foreign business community to water down the proposed legislation. Even in the face of this criticism, however, the foreign business community steadfastly maintained that its lobbying efforts were teaching China an important civics lesson about how laws were made in liberal democracies. More than one American lawyer made this point in interviews conducted during the time the legislation was being considered. (Not all of the lawyers interviewed seemed to appreciate the irony that they were "helping" Chinese citizens to appreciate the value of civic participation by opposing worker rights.)

It is truly remarkable that what one witnessed over an eighteen-month period between the time the law was proposed and passed very much resembled the kind of back and forth lobbying, argumentation, and public deliberation that one might expect in liberal democracy. Although in the overwhelming majority of cases the legislative process is driven by elites, the Chinese government was clearly and very deliberately experimenting with greater transparency and accountability by canvassing the views of interest groups and the greater public. Moreover, the legislative deliberations were highly nuanced and robust. Professor Zheng

Gongcheng, a member of the Standing Committee of the National People's Congress, observed to a Chinese-language magazine that the NPC was keenly aware that reconceptualizing labor relations was one of the most urgent tasks facing China in the reform era. "It attracted a lot of attention among the members during the considering and debating process," said Cheng. "Most members were competing to express their opinions, which had been a rare scene in the meeting of the Standing Committee."[60] Indeed, the biggest difference in how this might have played out in a true democracy was the virtual unanimity of the final vote which is typical of voting in China's national legislature. Despite the obviously bitter divisions and difficult compromises that had to be negotiated over an extended period, the new law received 145 (with one abstention) of the 146 votes cast by the Standing Committee of the National People's Congress.[61]

Fair Share, Moral Courage, and the Rule of Law

As we have seen, foreign business executives and the lawyers who represent them have made important contributions to the development of the rule of law in China, most notably through their insistence on transparency and providing input into the drafting of laws. However, these positive contributions go only as far as self-interest takes them and not an inch further. The drive for legal transparency and the movement to press the Chinese government on the enforcement of intellectual property were well-coordinated and vigorous efforts. The business community shrewdly sought safety and influence in numbers. They spoke through official collective channels such as the American and European Chambers of Commerce. However, when it comes to systemic legal issues that they do not perceive to be in their immediate self-interest, such as the development of an independent judiciary, the foreign business community and its lawyers have not shown such initiative and drive.

If only the economic interests of foreign companies were at stake, then one might regard their meager contribution to the rule of law in China as a private matter of little public or moral consequence. In fact, however, it would make a big difference to the development of the rule of law in

China if foreign companies were to show more backbone. To the extent that they attempt to resolve commercial disputes through the judicial system and insist on fairness and justice from that system, foreign business firms could positively influence the trajectory and pace of legal reform. Conversely, to the extent that foreign firms continue to rely on personalized power relations, foreign firms are slowing the emergence of the rule of law.

Specifically, there are three ways foreigners and their lawyers can make a difference. First, foreign companies can and should set a good example by showing some moral courage and conviction. Despite the aforementioned technical limitations to the ALL and the general obstacles to the rule of law, tens of thousands of ordinary Chinese citizens have used the ALL to sue the government.[62] The vast majority of these plaintiffs are poor and vulnerable. Yet they bravely challenge the government despite the potential for official retaliation. In one of the most enduring images from the 1989 Tiananmen Square massacre, a solitary, brave citizen stood in front of a column of tanks in defiance of government power. Today, Chinese citizens are not literally standing in front of a tank, but many of them are challenging government actions in courtrooms. What message does it send to these courageous citizens that very rich and powerful corporations are too afraid to use the legal system to protect their own rights?

A second way that foreigners can make a difference is by helping to bring greater professionalism and accountability to the administrative and judicial system. Although the passage and implementation of the ALL represents an important advance for the rule of law, scholars note that administrative arbitrariness persists, particularly in rural areas.[63] For example, in a study of ALL trials in Beijing, Shanghai, Chongqing, Wuhan, and Guangdong Province, Veron Mei-Ying Hung found that, despite the central Chinese government's avowals to curtail such practices, "interference, inter-court and intra-court influence, and bribery weaken the independence of the judiciary in administrative litigation."[64] By insisting on their WTO rights to fairness and impartiality in the judicial review of their administrative hearings and cases, foreigners can help to reduce this arbitrariness and promote consistency and predictability in the courts.

The individual Chinese citizen often represents herself in ALL lawsuits. Foreign companies, by contrast, can afford to pay some of the best lawyers in the world to fully vindicate their rights. One of the most fundamental building blocks of a rule of law is the idea of legal precedent or stare decisis. Once a court decides a legal principle, that case has weight in future cases that are the same or similar. By investing their substantial legal resources in the ALL system, foreign companies can help to develop a set of legal precedents for administrative review of government actions. Cases involving foreigners could serve as legal building blocks for cases involving ordinary Chinese citizens.

Ultimately, of course, the most effective assurance of fairness and justice in trials and administrative hearings is their conformance to a set of principles emanating from review by an independent judicial appeal process. Until trials and administrative hearings are subject to review by an independent judicial appellate branch, arbitrary rulings will continue to be issued. Here too foreign firms can make a difference. The rights of investors within China are not in fact legally determined simply by the whims of the Chinese party-state. By virtue of its membership in the WTO, China is obliged to uniform application of its laws and independent judicial review of its administrative rulings. By insisting on these rights, foreign corporations can foster the emergence of the rule of law.

To be sure, foreign companies could risk alienating government officials by resorting to administrative litigation. However, this is the same risk that ordinary Chinese citizens face every day when they bring administrative actions against the government. Bearing such risks is not too much to ask of foreign corporations. The point is not to suggest that foreign corporations should constantly be suing government officials or even to suggest that they should be doing it as often as they might in the United States. Litigation simply needs to be an option that is discussed in very unusual cases where some governmental unit is being unreasonable and blatantly violating the law.

Apart from their wealth and ability to hire the best lawyers money can buy, foreign companies have another advantage that the ordinary Chinese citizen does not have if they are unsuccessful in challenging government action—the support of international trade law. The specific lever for forcing China's compliance is the transitional review mechanism set up under the Accession Protocol pursuant to which the WTO may review China's compliance with the protocol for the first eight years of operation. Foreign companies can also utilize the WTO Dispute Settlement Body to pressure

China to implement an independent judicial review system. The problem with utilizing either of these levers is that since no company has actually tried to use the legal remedies available to them under Chinese law it will be impossible for trade regulators to argue that China is in any way violating its WTO commitments.

The third area in which foreign lawyers can make a difference is in supporting the professional independence and liberties of lawyers. The advocacy group Human Rights Watch has documented arrests, detention, harassment, and disbarment of lawyers representing unpopular or politically sensitive cases.[65] For example, in April 2008 the Ministry of Justice declined to renew the professional licenses of Teng Biao and Juang Tianyong, two lawyers who offered to represent Tibetans who were arrested for protesting in Lhasa. Sophie Richardson of Human Rights Watch declared that "Beijing is trying to intimidate the legal profession by suspending these two lawyers and threatening not to renew many licenses. The goals are to deter lawyers from representing human rights cases, and to deter firms from employing lawyers who want those cases."[66] Such attempts to intimidate lawyers and discourage them from taking unpopular cases ought to offend the ethical sensibilities of any lawyer. Foreign lawyers in China, if they acted collectively, can and should constitute an important force to protect the professional status of their Chinese colleagues.

Thus far, we have seen how foreign corporations and their lawyers can make a greater contribution to the rule of law. On what basis can we say that they should do so? The moral argument to do so can be derived from the "Fair Share" principles enunciated in chapter 1. Under certain circumstances, corporations have a duty to help ameliorate or remedy human rights violations perpetrated by others. In considering whether corporations have such a moral duty, three actor-specific factors should be taken into account: (1) the relationship of the corporation to the human rights victims (the closer the relationship, the stronger the duty); (2) the potential effectiveness of the corporation in promoting human rights (the greater the chance of being effective, the stronger the duty); and (3) the capacity of the corporation to withstand economic retaliation (the greater the capacity to withstand retaliation, the stronger the duty). Because we are here considering a moral duty to contribute to the fairness and independence of the legal system as a whole, rather than to any particular human rights victims with which Western corporations have specific contacts and relationships, it might be argued that the first criterion is not very strong as applied here. Nevertheless, the crucial contribution that multinational corporations can make and their substantial resources both would support a duty to help to develop the rule of law by fully exercising their legal rights.

The Fair Share principles also provide that the particular human rights duties of any one actor cannot be understood in isolation. The duties of each actor depend on the duties of other actors. All of these public, private, and nongovernmental actors have unique strengths and weaknesses or actor-specific criteria. In assessing how fair it is to ask multinational corporations to engage in upholding and promoting human rights, the Fair Share principles direct us to assess these strengths and weaknesses relative to those of other actors. To suggest that the foreign business community should begin to utilize the Chinese court system to resolve disputes with the Chinese government and that foreign lawyers in China should rally to support their local counterparts who are being intimidated by government officials for representing politically sensitive clients is merely to ask that foreigners do their "fair share" relative to other actors, no more and no less. Ordinary Chinese citizens are already bravely taking national, provincial, and local governments to court. National trade representatives and international trade institutions have negotiated and implemented important trade levers that could be used to promote greater human rights. Moreover, a number of NGOs such as the Ford Foundation, the American Bar Association, and academics both within and outside China have devoted extensive resources to tilling the soil for legal transformation in China. Every other actor with potential moral responsibility for promoting human rights in China has done their fair share. Only the business community and its lawyers have failed to do their part. They have failed to act, moreover, because they are afraid to risk their economic interest. While every day thousands of ordinary Chinese citizens, most unable to afford a lawyer, bravely press their grievances against the government in courtrooms, the foreign business community and its lawyers have chosen to ride in the "soft seat" on the road to legal reform. One can only hope that in the coming decade foreign firms and lawyers will find the moral courage to fulfill the very crucial role they can play in the development of the rule of law in China.

Apart from the moral argument, there is also a practical reason why it is in the long-term economic interest of the foreign business community to work more assiduously to develop the rule of law in China. There is something strangely inconsistent in a strategy of investing billions of dollars in a country where property rights are so ill defined and where the party-state can so easily adversely affect economic interests. The underlying logic and rationale for investing billions of dollars in a country such as China is that sometime in the next decade the political economy will develop to a point where property rights are secure. Yet multinational corporations that invest billions in China are not acting in a way that will help bring about a rights-respecting nation with an independent judiciary that upholds their economic rights.

One Western business executive with a prominent multinational company in China joked that "one thing you learn about due process in China is that there is none."[67] This blithe comment evinces the dangerous complacency of foreign companies and their lawyers in relying on exclusively non-legal, relationship-based means to protect their economic interests. They seem content to have China languish in the personalized, arbitrary system that defined the prereform era. This policy is self-defeating and on the wrong side of history. It is self-defeating because if the implicit assumption about the futile future of the rule of law in China is correct, the billions of dollars of capital invested in China will not be protected by secure property rights. If, conversely, the rule of law does emerge in China, then the foreign business community is on the wrong side of history. In any case, with so much at stake, the supposed wisdom of the foreign business community's legal timidity certainly warrants further reflection.

One indication that at least some elements of the foreign business community believe that occasionally challenging the Chinese government can be a viable business strategy is in a 2008 WTO case involving automobile parts by the United States, the European Union, and Canada. Foreign nations successfully argued that the Chinese government violated WTO provisions by discriminating against foreign auto parts in an effort to build up its domestic industry.[68] In November 2008, China settled another trade dispute with the United States, the European Union, and Canada by agreeing to allow financial information providers, such as Thomson Reuters, Dow Jones, and Bloomberg, to distribute financial news independently of the government-controlled Xinhua news agency.[69] As described in chapter 4, Western Internet companies are also considering addressing Chinese censorship as a trade issue.

The foregoing cases involve state-to-state claims in the WTO context. They have the backing of the U.S. government and/or the European Union. ALL actions, by contrast, would involve individual companies suing the particular branches or levels of the Chinese government in Chinese courts. Although such cases are unlikely to be as costly and momentous as a WTO dispute, they do involve going it alone. Thus, there is risk of retaliation. Nevertheless, the WTO cases suggest that some companies and industries do not believe they adequately pursue their economic interests in China simply by cultivating good *guanxi* with government officials, and have decided instead that the more prudent course is to press their legal rights. Similarly, Western companies and their lawyers may conclude that the risks of pursuing claims in Chinese courts are outweighed by the gains of solidifying their legal property rights. Certainly, even if individually companies may calculate that legal bravery is not worth the potential price of retaliation, it is in their collective interests to help establish legal protections for their economic rights.

What makes the behavior of Western companies and their lawyers all the more curious is that they are lending implicit moral support to this authoritarian system just as the rest of China is undergoing tectonic change and many brave Chinese citizens are risking life and liberty in attempting to move it in a progressive direction. Westerners seem content to be bystanders in this historic struggle going on within China, even though they have billions of dollars at stake in the struggle's outcome.

The experience of McDonald's provides an interesting cautionary tale about the long-term dangers of operating in China without a fair legal system. McDonald's has one thousand stores in China and employs sixty thousand workers, 40 percent of whom are students. In March 2007, investigative journalists from a local newspaper posed as students and obtained jobs working in McDonald's, Kentucky Fried Chicken, and Pizza Hut. The results of the investigation were published in the *New Express Daily*.

The headline that McDonald's was not paying minimum wage caused a firestorm of bad publicity for the company throughout China. The Guangdong Provincial Labor and Social Security Department demanded to inspect the employment records of all ninety-five McDonald's restaurants in Guangdong within seventy-two hours. The McDonald's lawyer with responsibility for labor relations in the Asia Pacific Region flew to Guangzhou and asked the local Chinese lawyer what a lawyer would normally ask when presented with such an onerous demand: "Is there any way to get a delay?" He was told in no uncertain terms that he would personally be arrested if the company did not comply. At about the same time the ACFTU started its own "investigation" of McDonald's and immediately declared McDonald's "guilty" of labor violations. Again, the lawyer representing McDonald's asked a simple question that any good lawyer would ask in this situation: "Who has the authority to decide this issue—the local Guangdong labor bureau or the ACFTU?"[70]

Eventually, what was threatening to spiral out of control as a public relations nightmare was resolved. After examining the records provided by McDonald's, the local Guangdong authorities exonerated McDonald's, finding that the wages paid by McDonald's to the undercover journalists were legal because they were in compliance with wage laws pertaining to students. However, the McDonald's incident illustrates how very little protection traditional notions of due process and the rule of law really offer to the property interests of foreign companies. The McDonald's incident should also serve as fair warning of what the next decade might bring for Western companies if as a result of the current global financial meltdown, China's economic expansion were to slow down significantly. In such a case, foreign companies will become juicy targets for government officials seeking to stoke nationalist sentiments. Western executives and their lawyers may one day wish that they had been more vigilant in asserting their property and due process rights and thereby helping to strengthen the rule of law in China.

6

Conclusion

The Two Chinas of 2020

After nearly three decades of explosive economic growth and accompanying tectonic social changes, China's future remains highly uncertain. This uncertainty has been heightened by the global financial meltdown that has reduced global demand for products manufactured by China's export-dependent economy. The issues examined in this book—working conditions, product safety, Internet freedom, and the rule of law—involve ongoing power struggles on a grand social scale. Many complex factors form the background for these struggles—growing economic inequality, regionalism, corruption, and a fledgling legal and regulatory system, to name but a few of the most important ones. In this concluding chapter I will consider how these diverse forces are likely to unfold in the coming decade, particularly in light of the new economic realities engendered by the global financial meltdown.

Enormous vested interests are at stake. For a start, there is the Communist Party's overarching desire to remain in power. This is not to say that Beijing is indifferent to the welfare of China's people. There are many dedicated and talented leaders in China, notwithstanding the tendency of many in the West to lump them all together as ruthless dictators. China would not have been able to achieve all that it has in the past three decades under incompetent leadership. However, there can be no denying that the Communist Party wants to continue to rule China and that it does not want any competition. Such absolute authoritarian ambitions can lead to decisions that are more about staying in power than about the public good.

The party-state is no longer the only political and social force in China, and its authoritarian grip will face increasingly potent challenges from a burgeoning civil society. When Deng Xiaoping began the process of economic reform three decades ago, change always started at the top. However, as we have seen in this book, the economic and political future of China is no longer solely dependent on opaque power struggles among political elites. The reform era has unleashed new voices and new sources of power in the emerging private sector—for example, a rapidly growing middle class that has yet to fully coalesce and define its political interests; workers who are grappling with the meaning and potential of new legal rights granted to them; and innumerable diverse and independent voices in the largest Internet community in the world. These and other forces make up what the historian Merle Goldman has called the transformation "from comrade to citizen."[1] In addition to enjoying greater personal freedoms in the private sphere, Chinese citizens are beginning to expect and sometimes demand greater accountability and performance from the party-state. As political scientist Dali Yang has written, this new dynamic requires the party-state to be "more efficient, more service-oriented, and more disciplined."[2]

It is tempting to imagine that the new relationship between citizen and state in China is leading ineluctably to a full-fledged democracy and respect for human rights. Seen in this light, China today might be viewed as in a pre-democratic state where the party-state needs to perform to remain legitimate and stay in power. Although the broad trends seem to point generally in such a progressive direction, this book has shown that powerful social forces could instead move China in another direction and that a democratic China is far from inevitable.

China is experiencing tremendous internal conflict and turmoil over the pace and direction of social and political change. The ultimate outcome of these struggles will depend on how issues such as those discussed in this book will be resolved. It is conceivable that instead of moving toward greater political freedom, China will regress into a tighter authoritarian grip. Not even China's continued rise as a global economic power is inevitable. If the social and political environments turn out badly, the economy will suffer too. Even if China does continue to grow in power and world stature, it is far from clear how it will exercise that power and prestige.

Questions That Will Determine China's Future

China's future depends largely on how Chinese citizens answer a panoply of questions. Will labor leaders be successful in establishing independent trade unions? Will local officials enforce existing labor laws? How pervasive will government corruption be? Will the All China Federation of Trade Unions evolve into a strong voice for worker rights? How quickly can China develop effective safety regulation for its manufacturing sector? Will Internet freedom continue to grow? Can Chinese citizens rely on the Internet for the news they need to be active and informed citizens? Or will government censorship become so tight and all pervasive that the informational and transformative value of the Internet will be all but choked off? Will activist lawyers be able to press environmental, housing, and other kinds of cases involving economic and civil rights? Will the judiciary evolve into an independent arbiter of the law? Or will the party-state continue to keep tight control over court deliberations and decisions? It is impossible to predict with certainty how any of these questions will be answered; the Chinese people will provide the answers as they address the historic challenges that await them in the coming decade.

Westerners, particularly businesspeople, also have a crucial role to play. The choices they make regarding worker rights, product safety, Internet freedom, and the rule of law will affect the pace and direction of social and political change in China. Among the key questions for the West are the following: Will brand-name companies implement effective worker-protection standards for their manufacturing subcontractors or will they, to minimize costs, turn a blind eye to labor abuses? Will foreign labor leaders foster or undermine the growth of independent trade unions? Will pharmaceutical companies help their Chinese supply chain to implement world-class safety and quality standards? Or will their pre-occupation with cost savings lead them to adopt a dangerous and cynical policy of accepting existing Chinese manufacturing standards? Will foreign Internet companies take a principled stand on censorship or will they continue to do as ordered by the party-state? Will foreign business test the waters in the Chinese legal system? Will they dare to resolve some disputes with the government through a legal rights approach? Or will they continue to pursue and protect their interests in China exclusively through friendly and personalized relations with government officials? In these and other areas Western business leaders have an opportunity to have a positive effect on the future of China. But they might as easily impede change. Will Western business executives have the vision and moral courage to influence China in a positive direction or will their contribution to history consist of a shortsighted acquiescence to more regressive forces?

This book leaves us with these and many more questions. The point of this book has not been so much to predict China's future as to understand the forces that will determine it. However, what is most striking when we do begin to reflect about how that future might look is the widely divergent range of possibilities that are likely to emerge. To appreciate how widely China's future can vary in the next decade, it is useful to imagine two Chinas in 2020. One, Pax China, has evolved out of the dark shadow of the Beijing Massacre. Westerners have helped China to move toward greater freedom, the rule of law, and business responsibility. The other, Nox China, remains in the shadow of Tiananmen. It is one in which Westerners have failed to act responsibly and remained passive bystanders or even enablers of a society that lurches toward a dysfunctional authoritarianism that threatens the continued viability of its economic reforms.

Pax China

Consider first the optimistic scenario of Pax China. A traveler to China in 2020 will witness a young and prosperous white-collar urban middle class. This group has moved beyond a fascination with automobiles and consumer goods. They are now settling down and raising families. They are worried about the air and water quality of their communities and about the quality of their schools. They pay taxes and constitute a powerful political force. They are unafraid to communicate their expectations to local and national political leaders who seek to be responsive to their expressed wishes. Many migrant workers have begun to prosper and put down roots in southern and coastal China. These areas have become stable and permanent residential communities with schools and hospitals.

By 2020, Chinese products will have acquired a global reputation for quality and reliability, as well as cost effectiveness. China's internal market has become so important that the country's prosperity is no longer so dependent on its export sector for growth. The Internet and private media outlets have made the free flow of information a way of life in China. Corruption, environmental degradation, and product safety are all subjects openly discussed on the Internet and elsewhere. Sunshine being the best disinfectant, the public discussion of these issues leads to progressive legal reforms.

Realistically, by 2020 the Communist Party will still be the only political party permissible in China, but the availability of public information and legal transparency will recast the relationship between the party and the society as one based increasingly on performance and accountability. There might be elections at the municipal and provincial level. Imagine an election for the mayor of Shanghai from among a slate of candidates put forth by the Party. Imagine provincial governors who share power with locally elected village and township leaders. Citizen disputes against one another and against government agencies will be decided by independent and professional judges. The judiciary may even on rare occasion be called upon to resolve constitutional disputes between different government agencies over which one possesses the authority on a given topic.

Pax China will project confidence and prosperity to the rest of the world. It will see Europe and the United States as rivals for global resources, prestige, and influence, but fundamentally its interests will be aligned around the need for global security and prosperity built on free trade and investment and military cooperation. Pax China will not be a clone of the United States or Europe. Culturally, Pax China will remain a unique country, very much evolving from its distinctive historical values. It will be a unique presence on the world stage but not a threatening or hostile one. Finally, as Pax China becomes more prosperous and democratic, the deep cultural ties with Taiwan will lead to serious talks about a peaceful reunification.

Nox China

Contrast the optimistic vision of Pax China with the pessimistic Nox China of 2020. Migrant workers in the south and on the east coast develop increasingly hostile relationships with factory operators. Because of corruption, local officials look the other way when labor violations occur. The ACFTU continues to suppress the formation of independent trade unions but it fails to develop into an authentic voice for the concerns of migrant workers. Violent labor disputes become more common and the ACFTU increasingly sides with local officials seeking to preserve stability and order.

The court system also continues to be heavily influenced by local party officials and lacks independence. Throughout Nox China people have lost confidence in the legal system as a means to resolve their disputes with each other and with the government. This further contributes to civil unrest. Concerned about rising unrest, the party-state tightens control over the Internet and the public dissemination of information. News and information travel slowly within Nox China. Product safety and quality fail to improve. Air and water pollution reach ever higher and more dangerous levels, further fostering discontent. Gradually, foreign companies have less and less appetite to invest in Nox China and manufacture products there.

To stay in power, Chinese leaders stoke nationalist pride and xenophobia. The Chinese economy fails to make a smooth transition from being export-driven to one with a large internal consumer market. As a result, unemployment among migrant workers and urban workers remains high. University graduates have great difficulty finding jobs. Nox China blames other countries for its economic woes. Some Chinese begin to characterize Western investment in Nox China as being similar to the foreign domination of the nineteenth and twentieth centuries. There is talk of renationalizing parts of the economy and reversing some economic reforms. A prosperous and democratic Taiwan has little interest in reunification. As Nox China stalls economically, however, the Taiwan issue becomes a lightning rod for channeling internal discontent. Nox China builds up its military and naval presence in the Taiwan Strait in a show of intimidating force.

Both of these dramatically different visions of China in 2020 are plausible. The prosperity and stability of what Fareed Zakaria has called the "Post-American World" will crucially depend on what kind of China emerges in the coming decade.[3] Clearly Pax China would foster global peace and prosperity, whereas Nox China would be risky and destabilizing. The future of China is a critical subject precisely because it is impossible to predict which of these two Chinas might emerge and yet the consequences are so momentous.

In the past three decades, economic reform has unleashed many necessary elements for a successful transition to a more open and democratic China that also respects human rights, but as we look forward to the next decade the ultimate outcome of this process remains highly uncertain. As this book has demonstrated, the actions and decisions of ordinary Chinese citizens and Westerners will determine which China emerges. When we speak of the future of China it is less instructive to speak of probabilities and predictions and more important to think about the internal forces and dynamics shaping that future and what Westerners can do to help point China along a positive path.

Muddling through the Middle Kingdom: Morality, Self-Interest, and the Dangers of Complacency

In this book I have argued that Western business has a moral duty to do its fair share to promote worker rights, product safety, Internet freedom, and the rule of law. However, enlightened self-interest should also motivate the business community to promote human rights and the rule of law. After three decades of economic reform, most Western business leaders have settled into a complacent relationship with the party-state, while all around them the political and social terrain moves beneath their feet. For many business leaders such acquiescence and accommodation seems the prudent course. This belief is premised on what might be termed a "muddling through" scenario for China's future.

The principal feature of the "muddling through" scenario when compared with Pax China and Nox China is stasis. Many Western business executives in China believe that change in China will occur very slowly. Liberty and human rights will expand in China, according to this view, but very slowly and in very small increments. Improvements in other areas such as government regulation and the rule of law will similarly be glacially slow and incremental. China 2020 will look pretty much the same as China 2010.

If the "muddling through" scenario is correct, then, at least on a practical, profit-maximizing level, the policy of not rocking the boat looks prudent. But how likely is China to "muddle through"? Change, indeed even radical change, seems a more likely bet than stasis. There is no reason to presume that the volatile social and political forces at work are going to cancel themselves out and result in a steady course of benign gradualism. They are more likely to be resolved more decisively into either the Pax or the Nox scenario. Continued economic growth and development simply isn't feasible unless China develops a high-quality and efficient manufacturing sector with a reputation for producing safe products. This, in turn, will not be possible unless there is a free business press to publicize problems, a capable regulatory system to enforce safety and quality standards, and an independent judiciary to enforce the law. Conversely, a China where the courts are unreliable and corrupt and where civil and labor strife is constantly breaking out in violent protest will not be one where property rights will be sufficiently secure for Western companies to continue to invest billions.

The recent global financial meltdown has revealed fissures in the Chinese economic model. As the United States and Europe entered into a liquidity crisis and credit crunch, demand for Chinese goods shrank. The effect on China was dramatic. By the beginning of 2009, 35 million workers were unemployed, with that number projected to rise to 50 million or 10 percent of non-agricultural workers. One-third (1.7 million of 5.6 million) of China's university graduates in 2008 were unable to find jobs.

In the short term, China and the West will need to work with each other to achieve a soft landing from the problems created by the collapse of the old economic paradigms. The United States will need China to continue to buy its debt securities. Conversely, it is in China's interest to continue to do so to prop up its most important export market. As China looks to the next (post-financial-meltdown) decade, however, the rules by which it achieved 10 percent growth for three decades no longer apply. Change in the form of economic restructuring is a necessity not an option.

To get back on track and create new jobs, China must restructure its economy in two crucial respects. First, it must reduce its dependence on foreign markets by developing a robust internal consumer market. Second, it must move up in global manufacturing class from T-shirts and sneakers to pharmaceuticals, automobiles, and aerospace. To build these kinds of new markets, China must successfully address the challenges described in this book—working conditions, product safety and quality, free flow of information, and the development of a reliable rule of law and system of property rights. Under the old economic paradigm of China supplying cheap products for credit-soaked foreign markets, some viewed these issues as obstacles to China's prosperity. Any discussion about such issues with Chinese leaders was likely to be viewed as unfriendly and contentious. In the next decade, however, these challenges, along with promoting environmentally sustainable growth, form the indispensable bedrock for continued prosperity. As a result, it is critical for both China and the West to find constructive ways of engaging on these issues. If China and Western business leaders fail to work together and make progress on these concerns, China will not be able to restructure its economy and it will certainly not be able to sustain the kind of growth it has enjoyed in the past three decades. This will not only be bad economic news for China and Western investors; because of the massive unemployment that will result, it will also place an enormous strain on China's social and political stability.

When Western business protects its investments and property interests by cultivating good relations with the party-state, it is in essence betting against its own long-term interests. Foreign investment can be secure and achieve returns for shareholders only when property rights are secure and protected by independent legal institutions. In a few rare cases such as the automobile parts, Internet, and financial news industries, Western companies have been willing to press claims against China through state-to-state WTO disputes. For the most part, however, Western business continues to eschew asserting its economic rights under Chinese or international law. Instead, these companies embrace cronyism and personalized relationships to protect their property interests, even as millions of brave Chinese citizens attempt to press their own claims against the government through the admittedly flawed and rudimentary legal system.

By clinging to precepts and presuppositions of authoritarian and clientalist China, Western business is on the wrong side of history. At best the muddling through scenario is the second best of three equally possible outcomes in China. Western business has so much to gain by avoiding Nox China and helping to move toward Pax China that it would be a serious mistake to presume the ironclad verity of muddling through in the Middle Kingdom and miss the historic opportunity to influence China toward a more sustainable social and political future.

Practicing "Tough Love"

How can a company that wants to operate profitably promote human rights, the rule of law, product safety, and democratic institutions in an authoritarian system in which criticism is not generally well received? Before considering some practicalities on how to engage in dialogue on these difficult issues, it is important to clarify that I am not suggesting that Western business executives should become broad critics of China's political system. Rather, I am arguing that they should play a constructive role in those areas in which they are directly involved. Companies manufacturing in China are responsible for how workers are treated. Internet companies have responsibilities when it comes to Internet freedom. Pharmaceutical companies have responsibilities for product safety. I am not calling on business leaders to engage in broad discussions about social and political issues with which they have no connection through their business practices. That said, in addition to assuring that safety and human rights are upheld in their own operations and those of their subcontractors, virtually every Western business has an interest in the development of the rule of law. Therefore, it is appropriate to expect that Western business adopt a broad proactive role in helping to improve the legal system.

How can Western businesspeople effectively engage government officials and ordinary citizens in discussions about controversial subjects while minimizing the potential negative impact on their business interests? One key is, where possible, to address issues through collective action. Shanghai, Beijing, and Hong Kong each have large and active chambers of commerce that provide forums for Western businesses to pool their resources and address issues of common concern. These organizations, as well as more narrow industrywide organizations based in Western countries (e.g., the Pharmaceutical Research and Manufacturers of America), are the channels through which Western businesses can most effectively and safely discuss controversial issues with Chinese officials. I am hopeful this book will inspire some members of these organizations to reconsider some of their short-sighted and self-defeating presuppositions about the best way to advance the long-term interests of Western business in China.

Besides acting through collective organizations, it is also critical for Western business to enlist the assistance of nongovernmental organizations that possess both technical expertise and clout with public opinion, at least outside of China. The Global Network Initiative organized by Western Internet companies offers a useful template for this sort of collaboration.

As we saw in chapter 4, however, the single most critical factor for Western business to engage effectively on social and political issues in China is the active participation of the United States and European governments. As the Western business community has settled into its complacent partnership with the Chinese party-state, the overwhelming preoccupation with trade and investment have crowded human rights and other difficult subjects off the agenda for Western governments in their dealings with China. Whereas, for example, under the Clinton administration the United States kept human rights issues in the forefront, even as it was welcoming China into the WTO, under the Bush administration, human rights and product safety issues have been ignored or bartered away in return for Chinese concessions on market access for financial and insurance businesses.

Time will tell how an Obama administration will balance the need to engage China on social and political issues with the other important military, geopolitical, and economic issues that make up the complicated relationship between the two countries. From the point of view of business, however, what this book has demonstrated is that it is a mistake for Western businesses to advocate that their national governments only speak softly, if at all, on social and political developments within China. This is precisely the kind of self-defeating policy that is on the wrong side of history in China and is not really in the long-term interest of business. Instead, Western business needs to understand that it can and should play a more constructive role in the social and political development of China, but that in order to do so effectively it cannot go it alone. Business needs the active, complementary support of Western governments. Western business and governments need together to rethink their stakes in China, what the potential outcomes are, and what they can and should do to influence those outcomes.

In addition to carefully selecting the institutional context for becoming engaged in internal Chinese affairs, the tone of discussion is critical. The resentment and hostility many Chinese feel over foreign criticism present a formidable challenge. Anyone who has ever tried to discuss a sensitive subject with a Chinese citizen understands how offended and defensive she might become when China is criticized. "You don't like

China and you are not our friend" is the instinctive response to criticism. Such reactions are deeply ingrained in the Chinese psyche—which isn't surprising in an authoritarian country where nationalist resentments are regularly stoked by the party-state. In this kind of environment, it is certainly understandable why foreign businesspersons in China are highly reluctant to become involved in discussions about China's social and political challenges.

One key toward engaging a difficult issue effectively with Chinese officials is to be able to practice "tough love," that is, to communicate forcefully but in a culturally sensitive manner and with a positive spirit that shows respect and admiration for China's many accomplishments and qualities. If one is going to raise a critical or sensitive issue, it is helpful to be very explicit about the fact that there is much to admire and respect about China and that one wishes only the best for the country and its people. Tom Gorrie is a former Johnson & Johnson executive who has traveled to the remotest parts of China and worked closely with government officials on a wide range of public policy issues, including health care, the environment, and currency issues. He is one of a handful of foreigners given the honor of carrying the Olympic torch on Chinese soil, in Tiananmen Square no less. "No one likes to be criticized," Gorrie says. "Chinese people are just tired of being criticized by foreigners. It doesn't mean you can't raise difficult issues and even challenge them a bit, but you have to be tactful and diplomatic. If you have established a relationship with them over time, have demonstrated an understanding of their issues, and are willing to work with them to find solutions to their issues, they will take your comments more seriously."[4]

John Kamm is a businessman who has been traveling to China for almost four decades. In 2004, Kamm was awarded a MacArthur Foundation "genius" award for his work with the Dui Hua Foundation, an NGO that he founded. Dui Hua has successfully intervened on behalf of hundreds of prisoners of conscience in China. Kamm regularly travels to China and meets with high-ranking government leaders, often raising extremely sensitive subjects with them. "In discussing sensitive issues like political prisoners with Chinese officials," Kamm says, "I have found that it is best to keep the meetings as low-key and informal as possible." Kamm also emphasizes that one of his major goals is to help China to be better understood and respected in the West. "Most important," says

Kamm, "I try to convince my counterparts that releasing someone that the government sees as an enemy holds benefits for China, being as specific as possible. I approach the enterprise with respect and in a spirit of friendship and trust. I am results oriented. I never criticize senior officials by name, and when the Chinese government does good, I find ways to recognize it."[5] Kamm's "tough love" approach of mixing friendship with criticism works. When journalist Tina Rosenberg asked Chinese officials about Kamm, one replied, "He loves China. He shows respect. He is constructive and realistic."[6]

In concluding, I am well aware that the role I envision for Western business executives challenges their most fundamental presuppositions about how to do business successfully in China and will thus require a sea change in their thinking. To date, partly for fear of souring friendly government relations, they have not regarded involvement in China's internal political and social matters as appropriate behavior or in their self-interest. On the contrary, they believe it is imprudent, foolish, and culturally insensitive to get involved in such thorny issues. They have even, again contrary to their true interests, discouraged Western political leaders from speaking out. However, as I have demonstrated in this book, for all of the risk of getting involved, there is even greater risk in not getting involved in shaping China's social and political future. The economic interests of Western business are in reality much more closely aligned with labor, environmental, legal, and human rights progress than Western business executives believe. In the coming decade and beyond, only a Pax China that protects civil and political rights will respect the economic rights of Western business. Complacency and inaction regarding civil and political rights in China thus could prove to be very costly. This is a case where doing well and doing good overlap. Western business can—and should—do more to influence social and political change in China.

NOTES

1. Beyond the Shadow of Tiananmen

1. "'Inflation' Beats 'Corruption' to Top of Public Concerns," *China Daily,* January 24, 2008.

2. Pew Research Center, Global Attitudes Project Report, *The Chinese Celebrate Their Roaring Economy, as They Struggle with Its Costs,* July 22, 2008.

3. See Bruce Russett, *Grasping the Democratic Peace* (Princeton 1994). For an alternative view, see Jack Snyder, *From Voting to Violence: Democratization and Nationalist Conflict* (Norton 2000). See generally Fareed Zakaria, *The Future of Freedom: Illiberal Democracy at Home and Abroad,* rev. ed. (Norton 2007).

4. State Council of the People's Republic of China "White Paper," *Human Rights in China* (November 1991). See generally Ann Kent, *Between Freedom and Subsistence: China and Human Rights* (Oxford 1993).

5. David Shambaugh, "China's Competing Nationalisms," *International Herald Tribune,* May 5, 2008.

6. Susan Shirk, *China: Fragile Superpower: How China's Internal Politics Could Derail Its Peaceful Rise* (Oxford 2007).

7. Confidential author interview, New York, May 5, 2008.

8. Ibid.

9. Ibid.

10. Ibid.

11. Ibid.

12. James Reidel et al., *How China Grows: Investment, Finance, and Reform* (Princeton 2007).

13. Ibid.

14. For a discussion of the various social safety net challenges facing China as it transitions to a market economy, see C. Fred Bergsten et al., *China: The Balance Sheet* (Public Affairs 2006).

15. See, e.g., A. M. Rosenthal, "Meeting at Tiananmen," *New York Times*, June 4, 1999. For a more recent argument that economic engagement is perpetuating an authoritarian regime, see James Mann, *The China Fantasy: How Our Leaders Explain Away Chinese Repression* (Viking 2007).

16. See, e.g., U.S.-China Business Council, "China PNTR: Advancing America's Values," April 26, 2000, http://www.uschina.org/public/wto/usavalues.html.

17. Doug Guthrie, *Dragon in a Three Piece Suit* (Princeton 1999), 194. See also Daniel Rosen, *Behind the Open Door: Foreign Enterprises in the Chinese Marketplace* (Institute for International Economics 1999).

18. Michael A. Santoro, *Profits and Principles: Global Capitalism and Human Rights in China* (Cornell 2000), 70–71.

19. Mary Elizabeth Gallagher, *Contagious Capitalism: Globalization and the Politics of Labor in China* (Princeton 2005), 28.

20. Bruce J. Dickson, *Red Capitalists in China: The Party, Private Entrepreneurs, and Prospects for Political Change* (Cambridge 2003), 159. See also Margaret M. Pearson, "Entrepreneurs and Democratization in China's Foreign Sector," in *New Entrepreneurs of Europe and Asia: Patterns of Development in Russia, Eastern Europe, and China*, ed. V. E. Bonnell and T. B. Gold (M. E. Sharpe 2002), 130–55.

21. Some legal scholars and activists are attempting to find ways to turn corporate moral responsibilities into legal obligations. See generally David Weissbrodt and Maria Kruger, "Norms on the Responsibilities of Transnational Corporations and Other Business Enterprises with Regard to Human Rights," *American Journal of International Law* 97, no. 4 (2003), 901. John Ruggie, the United Nations special representative for business and human rights, has issued a report that, among other things, recommends that nation-states encourage a rights-respecting corporate culture by requiring annual sustainability reports and making a corporation's "policies, rules, and practices" relevant factors in claims of corporate criminal accountability and punishment. *Protect, Respect and Remedy: A Framework for Business and Human Rights*, A/HRC/8/5, April 7, 2008, http://www.business-humanrights.org/Documents/RuggieHRC2008. See also John Ruggie, "Business and Human Rights: The Evolving International Agenda," 101 *American Journal of International Law* 101 (2007): 819. See generally Steven R. Ratner, "Corporations and Human Rights: A Theory of Responsibility," *Yale Law Journal* 111 (2001): 443.

22. Some philosophers question the fundamental premise that corporations can be thought of as persons that have moral obligations in the same way that individuals do. See generally Peter French, "The Corporation as a Moral Person," *American Philosophical Quarterly* 16, no. 3 (1979): 207–15. Economists too have their misgivings, dating back to Milton Friedman, who famously wrote in a *New York Times Magazine* article that the "sole responsibility of business is to increase its profits." Better to leave solutions of social problems to governments that represent the will of the people, thought Friedman. Milton Friedman, "The Social Responsibility of Business Is to Increase Profits," *New York Times Magazine*, September 13, 1970.

23. See generally Thomas Donaldson and Thomas W. Dunfee, *Ties That Bind: A Social Contract Approach to Business Ethics* (Harvard Business School Press 1999).

24. Among philosophers there is considerable debate about many aspects of human rights. Controversial issues include whether there is a sound philosophical basis for claiming that human rights exist, whether invoking human rights is the best way to protect the interests they are intended to protect, and which matters deserve to be on the list of rights that qualify as human rights. See generally Jeremy Waldron, "The Role of Rights in Practical Reasoning: 'Rights'

versus 'Needs,'" *Journal of Ethics* 4 (2000): 115, and Maurice Cranston, *What Are Human Rights?* (Taplinger 1973).

25. For an overview of the relationship of human rights to state sovereignty, see Jack Donnelly, *Universal Human Rights in Theory and in Practice,* 2nd ed. (Cornell 2002).

26. See Oliver F. Williams, "A Lesson from the Sullivan Principles: The Rewards for Being Proactive," in *Global Codes of Conduct: An Idea Whose Time Has Come,* ed. Oliver F. Williams (Notre Dame 2000).

27. In the case of "negative" rights such as the right to free speech the basic correlative duty consists of not violating the right at issue. The question of correlative duties becomes more complicated in the case of "positive" rights such as the right to education. In such cases one must ask who exactly must affirmatively provide the resources needed to make that right a reality. See Henry Shue, *Basic Rights,* 2nd ed. (Princeton 1996), and James W. Nickel, *Making Sense of Human Rights* (California 1987).

28. See also Michael A. Santoro, *Profits and Principles,* note 7, esp. 143–58.

2. The Clipboard, the Megaphone, and Socialist Characteristics

1. Compare, e.g., D. Card and A. B. Krueger, *Myth and Measurement: the Economics of the Minimum Wage* (Princeton 1995) (arguing that the minimum wage has modest impacts on employment numbers), with D. Neumark and W. Wascher, "Minimum Wage Effects on School and Work Transitions of Teenagers," *American Economic Review* 85, no. 2 (2004): 244–49 (arguing that increasing the minimum wage and raising labor standards increases unemployment).

2. Compare D. G. Arnold and N. E. Bowie, "Sweatshops and Respect for Persons," *Business Ethics Quarterly* 13, no. 2 (2003): 221–42 (arguing that forced overtime represents immoral coercion), with Gordon G. Sollars and Fred Englander, "Sweatshops: Kant and Consequences," *Business Ethics Quarterly* 17, no. 1 (2007): 115–33 (arguing that forced overtime is a morally acceptable term of the employment contract).

3. See Christopher McCrudden and Anne Davies, "A Perspective on Trade and Labor Rights," *Journal of International Economic Law* 3, no. 1 (2000); Chantal Thomas, "Should the World Trade Organization Incorporate Labor and Environmental Standards?" *Washington & Lee L. Review* 61 (2004): 347. See generally Kevin Kolben, "Integrative Linkage: Combining Public and Private Regulatory Approaches in the Design of Trade and Labor Regimes," *Harvard International Law Journal* 48, no. 1 (2007): 203.

4. The term "corporate social responsibility" has a much broader meaning than simply exercising responsibility for working conditions in the supply chain, but that term is used in this chapter because this is how the majority of people involved in the antisweatshop movement use it. In its broader meaning, CSR can include such diverse practices as corporate philanthropy, community investment, and adherence to environmental principles. See Cynthia A. Williams and Ruth V. Aguilera, "Corporate Social Responsibility in a Comparative Perspective," in *The Oxford Handbook of Corporate Social Responsibility,* ed. A. Crane et al. (Oxford 2008).

5. World Bank, *World Development Report 2008.*

6. Albert Keidel, "The Limits of a Smaller, Poorer China," *Financial Times,* November 13, 2007.

7. See Ariana Eunjung Cha "China Passes Germany with 3rd Highest GDP," *Washington Post,* January 15, 2009.

8. For the official poverty line designation in the United States, see *Federal Register* 74, no. 14 (January 23, 2009): 4199–4201.

9. Yang Xi, "Wealth Gap Demands Close Attention," http://www.china.org.cn/english/China/238582.htm (accessed February 20, 2008).

10. Author interview, February 13, 2008.

11. Peter Day, "Rural Poor Struggle on in China," *BBC News,* February 16, 2008.

12. Howard W. French, "Lives of Grinding Poverty, Untouched by China's Boom," *New York Times,* January 13, 2008.

13. Pun Ngai, *Made in China: Women Factory Workers in a Global Workplace* (Duke 2005), 65.

14. See generally Ching Kwan Lee, *Against the Law: Labor Protests in China's Rustbelt and Sunbelt* (California 2007); Mary Gallagher, *Contagious Capitalism: Globalization and the Politics of Labor in China* (Princeton 2005); and Anita Chan, *China's Workers under Assault: The Exploitation of Labor in a Globalizing Economy* (East Gate 2001).

15. For an analysis of the difference between confrontational and cooperative NGOs, see Michael A. Santoro, "Defending Labor Rights: On the Barricades and in the Boardroom," *Brown Journal of World Affairs* 8, no. 2 (2003).

16. T. A. Frank, "Confessions of a Sweatshop Inspector," *Washington Monthly,* May 1, 2008.

17. SACOM, public statement on the Walt Disney Company annual meeting of shareholders, March 6, 2008.

18. National Labor Committee, *A Wal-Mart Christmas: Brought to You by a Sweatshop in China* (December 2007).

19. Jonathan Dee, "A Toy Maker's Conscience," *New York Times Magazine,* December 23, 2007.

20. See generally Michael A. Santoro, "Beyond Codes of Conduct and Monitoring: An Organizational Integrity Approach to Global Labor Practices," *Human Rights Quarterly* 25, no. 2 (May 2003).

21. Richard Locke et al., "Does Monitoring Improve Labor Standards? Lessons from Nike," *Industrial and Labor Relations Review* 61, no. 1 (October 2007).

22. *Southern Weekend,* December 2005, http://www.southcn.com/weekend/economic/2005 12150038.htm (accessed February 12, 2008).

23. Frank, "Confessions of a Sweatshop Inspector."

24. Dan McDougall, "*Observer* Story Prompts Clothing Giant's Pledge," *Observer,* November 4, 2007.

25. Jonathan Dee, "A Toy Maker's Conscience."

26. See generally Santoro, "Defending Labor Rights."

27. Editorial, *Asian Labor Update,* July–September 2006.

28. Author interview, January 7, 2008.

29. Reuters, "China Brickwork Slave Children May Number 1,000," June 15, 2007.

30. Author interview, May 24, 2006, Beijing.

31. "Huawei Drops Resignation Scheme," *China Daily,* November 12, 2007.

32. Confidential author interviews, January 12, 2007. Mr. Chen and Mr. Wu are fictitious names.

33. "ACFTU: Neither a Partner Nor a Counterpart," *Asian Labor Update* (April–June 2006).

34. Comments of Vice Chairman Li, Hubei Province ACFTU, Cornell School of Labor and Industrial Relations, New York City, November 29, 2007.

35. "China President Ordered Wal-Mart Union Campaign," *Dow Jones Newswire,* August 16, 2006.

36. Mei Fong and Kris Maher, "U.S. Labor Leader Aided China's Wal-Mart Coup," *Wall Street Journal,* June 22, 2007.

37. Xiaodan Zhang, "Trade Unions and Paternalistic Rule in Today's China," unpublished manuscript available from author at xzhang@york.cuny.edu; Mingwei Liu, "Chinese Employment Relations and Trade Unions in Transition," Ph.D. dissertation, Cornell University (2009).

38. "ACFTU: Neither a Partner Nor a Counterpart."

39. Author interview, January 9, 2008.

40. Confidential author interview, January 10, 2008.

41. John Ruwitch and Lindsay Beck, "China Migrant Workers Learn the Law to Win Rights," *Reuters,* March 1, 2008.

42. Tim Beaty, comments made at the Murphy Institute for Worker Education and Labor Studies at the City University of New York, May 5, 2008.

43. Jon Hiatt, "A Snapshot of China's Labor Landscape: Delegation of AFL-CIO General Counsels Visits China," comments made at the Murphy Institute for Worker Education and Labor Studies at the City University of New York, May 5, 2008.

44. John Vandaele, "International Union Sets Up China Links," International Press Service, January 22, 2008.

3. Drug Safety Races to the Bottom

1. Jonathan D. Rockoff, "Maryland Native's Expertise Led to Drug Recall," *Baltimore Sun,* March 13, 2008.

2. See Carter Dougherty and Elisabeth Rosenthal, "Germans Seek China Tie to Blood Thinner Heparin," *New York Times,* March 8, 2008. See also Jeanne Whalen, Thomas M. Burton, and Anna Wilde Mathews, "Three More European Countries Recall Heparin," *Wall Street Journal,* March 26, 2008.

3. Walt Bogdanich, "Chinese Chemicals Flow Unchecked onto World Drug Market," *New York Times,* October 31, 2007.

4. Walt Bogdanich and Jake Hooker, "From China to Panama, a Trail of Poisoned Medicine," *New York Times,* May 6, 2007.

5. Walt Bogdanich and Jake Hooker, "Battle against Counterfeit Drugs Has New Weapon: Pollen," *New York Times,* February 12, 2008.

6. Jane Zhang and Alicia Mundy, "U.S. Restricts China Milk Products," *Wall Street Journal,* November 14, 2008.

7. Jake Hooker and Walt Bogdanich, "Tainted Drugs Linked to Maker of Abortion Pill," *New York Times,* January 31, 2008.

8. See U.S. Consumer Product Safety Commission, *Import Safety Strategy* (July 2008).

9. "Poisoned Gyoza Cases Prompt Japanese Firms to Seek Alternatives to Chinese Imports," NikkeiNet Interactive, March 12, 2008, http://www.nni.nikkei.co.jp/FR/FEAT/poison_gyoza/ (accessed March 19, 2008).

10. Wei Zhang and Xue Liu, "Challenges To China's Pharmaceutical Industry and Policy Implications," in *Prescribing Cultures and Pharmaceutical Policy in the Asia Pacific,* ed. Karen Eggleston (Forthcoming, Brookings 2009).

11. Author interview, March 24, 2008.

12. Hongzhang Yin, "Regulations and Procedures for New Drug Evaluation and Approval in China," *Human Gene Therapy* (October 2006): 970.

13. Bogdanich, "Chinese Chemicals Flow Unchecked onto World Drug Market."

14. See Beth Lloyd, *Are Chinese Drugs and Chemicals Safe?* http://blogs.abcnews.com/ theworldnewser/2007/10/are-chinese-dru.html (accessed November 15, 2007).

15. "MOH Will Oversee Food, Drug Safety," *China Daily,* March 12, 2008.

16. Shan Juan, "Tighter Controls on Drug Firms in China," *China Daily,* April 9, 2008.

17. Bogdanich, "Chinese Chemicals Flow Unchecked onto World Drug Market."

18. Confidential author interview, November 14, 2007.

19. Andrew Jacobs, "Parents Reject China Milk Settlement, *New York Times,* January 14, 2009. See generally George W. Conk, "People's Republic of China Civil Code: Tort Liability Law," *Fordham Law Legal Studies Research Paper No. 892432* (December 2005), http://papers.ssrn.com/ sol3/papers.cfm?abstract_id=892432.

20. Author interview, November 16, 2008.

21. Anna Wilde Mathews and Thomas M. Burton, "China Plant Played Role in Drug Tied to 4 Deaths," *Wall Street Journal,* February 14, 2008.

22. Anna Wilde Mathews, "FDA's Scrutiny of Drug Makers Abroad Faulted," *Wall Street Journal,* November 2, 2007.

23. Joseph Acker, "A Call for FDA Inspections," *Pharmaceutical Technology,* September 2007.

24. Kerry Capell, "A Drug Watchdog to Rival the FDA," *Business Week,* February 28, 2005.

25. Ibid.

26. "FDA Foreign Drug Inspection Program: A System at Risk," Subcommittee on Oversight and Investigations of the Committee on Energy and Commerce, November 1, 2007.

27. Statement of Guy Villax, "FDA Foreign Drug Inspection Program," Committee on House Energy and Commerce Subcommittee on Oversight and Investigations, November 1, 2007.

28. Gregory Lopes, "U.S., China Work toward Safety," *Washington Times,* December 5, 2007.

29. Jason Leow and Jane Zhang, "Product-Safety Pacts Put Greater Burden on Beijing," *Wall Street Journal,* December 12, 2007.

30. Jake Hooker and Walt Bogdanich, "Agreement with China to Regulate Some Drugs," *New York Times,* December 12, 2007.

31. Elaine Kurtenbach, "China SFDA: Buyers Must Vet Drug Safety," Associated Press, February 27, 2008.

32. See Michael J. Trebilock and Robert Howse, *The Regulation of International Trade,* 3rd ed. (Routledge 2005), 202–31.

33. Author interview, November 15, 2008.

34. Jean-François Tremblay, "Sourcing from China," *Chemical & Engineering News* 86, no. 20 (May 19, 2008): 15–20.

35. Confidential author interview, March 29, 2008.

36. Author interview, March 12, 2008.

37. Tremblay, "Sourcing from China."

38. Ibid.

39. Mathews and Burton, "China Plant Played Role in Drug Tied to 4 Deaths."

40. David Barboza and Walt Bogdanich, "Twists in Chain of Supply for Blood Drug," *New York Times,* February 28, 2008.

41. Jennifer Corbett Dooren, "FDA Identifies Contaminant Found in Baxter's Heparin," *Wall Street Journal,* March 19, 2008.

42. See generally *Gaines-Tabb v. ICI Explosives USA, Inc.,* 160 F.3d 613 (10th Cir. 1998).

43. "Building Biomanufacturing Capacity: The Chapter and Verse," *Nature Biotechnology* 24, no. 5 (2006): 503–5.

44. Author interview, April 11, 2008.

45. Ibid.

46. Ibid.

47. "Agencies Seek Ways to Create Drug-Tracking System," *Washington Drug Letter* 40, no. 12 (March 24, 2008).

4. China 2.0

1. BBC, "Surge in Chinese Internet Users," January 14, 2009.

2. JuxtConsult, "India's Internet Users Reach 30 Million," http://www.marketingcharts.com/interactive/indias-Internet-users-reach-30-million-637/ (accessed April 14, 2008).

3. Internet censorship is not limited to China. See Ronald Deibert et al., eds., *Access Denied: The Practice and Policy of Global Internet Filtering* (MIT 2008); and Jack Goldsmith and Tim Wu, *Who Controls the Internet: Illusions of a Borderless World* (Oxford 2006).

4. For a description of the technical details of how China uses network switches to censor foreign websites, see James Fallows, "The Connection Has Been Reset," *Atlantic Monthly,* March 2008.

5. Paul Wiseman, "In China, a Battle over Web Censorship," *USA Today,* April 23, 2008, A1.

6. Internet Society of China, "Public Pledge of Self Regulation and Professional Ethics for China Internet Industry," http://www.isc.org.cn/20020417/ca102762.htm (accessed April 22, 2008).

7. Reporters Without Borders, *China: Journey to the Heart of Internet Censorship* (October 2007).

8. Ibid. See generally Rebecca MacKinnon, "China's Censorship 2.0: How Companies Censor Blogs," *First Monday* 14, no. 2, February 2, 2009.

9. Wiseman, "In China, a Battle over Web Censorship."

10. Jim Yardley, "Chinese Nationalism Fuels Crackdown on Tibet," *New York Times,* March 31, 2008, A1.

11. See PEN website, http://www.pen.org/viewmedia.php/prmMID/1841/prmID/172 (accessed April 20, 2008).

12. Fallows, "The Connection Has Been Reset."

13. The survey by media company IAC and ad agency JWT was reported in Geoffrey A. Fowler, "Bloggers in China Start Testing Limits of 'Mental Firewall'," *Wall Street Journal,* December 5, 2007.

14. Bruce Einhorn, "China: Falling Hard for Web 2.0," *BusinessWeek Online,* January 15, 2007.

15. China Journal blog, "Torch Today: Quake Brings Calls for Relay's End," *Wall Street Journal Online,* May 13, 2008, http://blogs.wsj.com/chinajournal/2008/05/13/torch-today-quake-brings-calls-for-relays-end/.

16. Susan Jakes, "Hostages of the State," *Time,* June 16, 2003.

17. Sophie Beach, "The Rise of Rights," *China Digital Times,* May 27, 2005, http://chinadigitaltimes.net/2005/05/rise-of-rights/ (accessed October 24, 2008).

18. "Freed Prisoner Shows Legal System's Flaws," *China Daily,* April 6, 2005.

19. Benjamin L. Liebman and Tim Wu, "China's Network Justice" (January 9, 2007), *Columbia Public Law Research Paper No. 07–143,* http://ssrn.com/abstract=956310.

20. Andrew Jacobs, "To the Rescue, Uncensored," *New York Times,* May 14, 2008, A1.

21. See http://zm32869.bokeee.com/viewdiary.15983430.html (accessed July 15, 2007).

22. See http://abang.bokee.com/index.html (accessed July 15, 2007).

23. Xiao Qiang, "The 'Blog' Revolution Sweeps across China," *New Scientist,* November 24, 2004.

24. Rebecca Mackinnon, "The Chinese Censorship Foreigners Don't See," *Wall Street Journal Asia,* August 14, 2008.

25. Naomi Li, "Tackling China's Water Crisis Online," *China Dialogue,* September 21, 2006.

26. Ibid.

27. Jonathan Watts, "The Man Making the World's Worst Polluter Clean Up Its Act," *Observer,* July 8, 2007.

28. Howard W. French, "Great Firewall of China Faces Online Rebels," *New York Times,* February 4, 2008.

29. Clive Thompson, "Google's China Problem," *New York Times Magazine,* April 23, 2006.

30. Robert A. Guth, "Microsoft Revises Policy on Shutting Down Blogs," *Wall Street Journal,* February 1, 2006.

31. Benjamin Pimentel, "Alibaba Looking to Buy Back Yahoo Stake," *Marketwatch,* March 19, 2008.

32. Thompson, "Google's China Problem," April 23, 2006.

33. Quoted in Tom Zeller Jr., "Online Firms Facing Questions about Censoring Internet Searches in China," *New York Times,* February 15, 2006.

34. See Henry Shue, *Basic Rights,* 2nd ed. (Princeton University Press 1996), and James W. Nickel, *Making Sense of Human Rights* (University of California Press, 1987).

35. George Brenkert, "Google, Human Rights, and Moral Compromise," *Journal of Business Ethics* 80 (2008). See also Jeffery D. Smith, "Internet Content Providers and Complicity in Human Rights Abuse," in *Ethical Theory and Business,* 8th ed., ed. Tom Beauchamp, Norman Bowie, and Denis Arnold (Prentice Hall 2008).

36. In recent years activist lawyers in the United States have attempted to use the Alien Tort Claims Act of 1789 (ATCA) to hold companies with operations in the United States liable for torts committed against citizens of foreign countries. In 2007, a federal appeals court held that the ATCA could be used by victims of apartheid against corporations that supplied the apartheid government with equipment and other means to carry out its repression. *Khulumani v. Barclay National Bank, Ltd.,* 504 F.3rd 254 (2007). Because of the large number of financial conflicts of interest that its members had, the Supreme Court declined to hear an appeal of the decision. See Linda Greenhouse, "Conflicts for Justices Halt Appeal in Apartheid Case," *New York Times,* May 13, 2008.

37. Elliott Schrage, "Testimony of Google Inc. before the Subcommittee on Asia and the Pacific, and the Subcommittee on Africa, Global Human Rights, and International Operations," February 15, 2006.

38. Human Rights Watch, *Race to the Bottom: Corporate Complicity in Chinese Internet Censorship* (2006).

39. Brenkert, "Google, Human Rights, and Moral Compromise."

40. See Gary Clyde Hufbauer, Jeffrey Schott, and Kimberly Anne Elliot, *Economic Sanctions Reconsidered: History and Current Policy* (Institute for International Economics 1990).

41. See http://www.globalnetworkinitiative.org/.

42. Letter from Michael Samway, vice president and deputy general counsel, Yahoo! Inc., to Senators Richard Durbin and Tom Coburn, August 1, 2008.

43. See generally Tim Wu, "The World Trade Law of Internet Filtering" (May 3, 2006), http://ssrn.com/abstract=882459.

44. Eric Bangerman, "EU May Begin Treating 'Net Censorship as a Trade Barrier," http://arstechnica.com/news.ars/post20080227 (accessed July 22, 2008).

45. Bloomberg L.P. Press Release, November 13, 2008.

46. See Michael A. Santoro, *Profits and Principles: Global Capitalism and Human Rights in China* (Cornell 2000), 72–94.

47. See Surya Deva, "Corporate Complicity in Internet Censorship in China: Who Cares for the Global Compact or the Global Online Freedom Act?" *George Washington International Law Review* 39 (2007): 255–319; http://ssrn.com/abstract=964478.

48. The text of President Clinton's speech can be found at http://news.bbc.co.uk/2/hi/asia-pacific/122320.stm.

49. See PBS, "Stern Words for China," November 16, 2008, http://www.pbs.org/newshour/bb/asia/july-dec05/bush_11–16.html.

50. See David E. Sanger and Joseph Kahn, "Chinese Leader Gives Bush a Mixed Message," *New York Times,* November 21, 2005.

5. Soft Seat on the Long March

1. For a discussion of the various social-safety-net challenges facing China as it transitions to a market economy, see C. Fred Bergsten et al., *China: The Balance Sheet* (Public Affairs 2006).

2. See Martin K. Whyte and William L. Parish, *Urban Life in Contemporary China* (University of Chicago Press 1984); Andrew Walder, *Communist Neo-Traditionalism: Work and Authority in Chinese Industry* (University of California Press 1986).

3. Da Chen, *Colors of the Mountain* (Anchor/Random House 1999).

4. For a description of the increasing importance of merit in salaries and promotions in the Chinese economy, see Michael A. Santoro, *Profits and Principles: Global Capitalism and Human Rights in China* (Cornell 2000), 47–56.

5. See Randall Peerenboom, *China's Long March toward the Rule of Law* (Cambridge 2002).

6. See generally Neil J. Diamant, Stanley B. Lubman, and Kevin J. O'Brien, "Law and Society in the People's Republic of China," in *Engaging the Law in China: State, Society, and Possibilities for Justice*, ed. Neil J. Diamant et al. (Stanford 2005).

7. Stanley B. Lubman, *Bird in a Cage: Legal Reform in China after Mao* (Stanford 1999).

8. Ibid.

9. For an overview of the CCP and Chinese politics, see Kenneth Lieberthal, *Governing China: From Revolution though Reform,* 2nd ed. (Norton 2003); for one account of what China's government might look like in coming decades, see Bruce Gilley, *China's Democratic Future: How It Will Happen and Where It Will Lead* (Columbia 2004).

10. Benjamin L. Liebman, "China's Courts: Restricted Reform," in *China's Legal System: New Developments, New Challenges,* ed. Donald C. Clarke (Cambridge 2008).

11. Quoted in Veron Mei-Ying Hung, "China's WTO Commitment on Independent Judicial Review: Impact on Legal and Political Reform," *American Journal of Comparative Law* 52 (2004): 77, 124.

12. Jerome A. Cohen, "A Just Legal System," *International Herald Tribune,* December 11, 2007.

13. Quotes in paragraph culled from Chinese media and reported in Willy Lam, "The CCP Strengthens Control over the Judiciary," *China Brief* 8, no. 14 (July 3, 2008).

14. Human Rights Watch, Press Release, "Indonesia: Bold Court Decision Good for Free Expression," July 19, 2007.

15. Diamant, Lubman, and O'Brien, "Law and Society in the People's Republic of China," 6–7.

16. Li Li, "Come See, Come Sue," *Beijing Review,* December 21, 2006.

17. Simon Montlake, "Aggrieved Chinese Citizens Discovering the Lawsuit," *Christian Science Monitor,* August 2, 2007.

18. Minxin Pei, *China's Trapped Transition: The Limits of Developmental Autocracy* (Harvard 2006).

19. Carl F. Minzer, "Xinfang: An Alternative to Formal Chinese Legal Institutions," 42 *Stanford Journal of International Law* 103 (2006).

20. Zhonghua Renmin Gongheguo Xingzheng Susong Fa, promulgated on April 4, 1989, and effective on October 1, 1990.

21. See Randall Peerenboom, "Globalization, Path Dependency, and the Limits of the Law: Administrative Law Reform and the Rule of Law in the People's Republic of China," 19 *Berkeley Journal of International Law* 1 (2001); Jianfu Chen, *Chinese Law: Toward an Understanding of Chinese Law, Its Nature and Development* (Kluwer 1999); Donald Clarke, "China's Legal System and the WTO: Prospects for Compliance," *Washington University Global Studies Law Review* 2 (2003), 97.

22. WTO, *Report of the Working Party on the Accession of China,* WT/ACC/CHN/49 (October 1, 2001) ["Working Party Report"]; WTO, *Accession of the People's Republic of China,* WT/L/432 (November 10, 2001) ["Accession Protocol"].

23. A 2005 United States Trade Representative report characterized China's services-sector commitments as "far-reaching, particularly when compared to the services commitments of many other WTO members." United States Trade Representative, *2005 Report to Congress on China's WTO Compliance,* http://www.ustr.gov/assets/Document_Library/Reports_Publications/2005/asset_upload_file293_8580.pdf, 74; see generally, Karen Halverson, "China's WTO Accession: Economic, Legal, and Political Implication," *Boston College International and Comparative Law Review* 27, no. 2 (2004): 319–70.

24. General Agreement on Tariffs and Trade, October 30, 1947, 61 Stat. A-11, 55 U.N.T.S. 194, Art. X(3)(a).

25. Agreement on Trade-Related Aspects of Intellectual Property Rights, April 15, 1994, Marrakech Agreement Establishing the World Trade Organization, Annex 1C, Legal Instruments—Results of the Uruguay Round, 33 I.L.M. 81 (1994).

26. Article VI (2) (b) of the GATS offers an intriguing qualification that this requirement "shall not be construed to require a Member to institute such tribunals or procedures where this would be inconsistent with its constitutional structure or the nature of its legal system."

27. Accession Protocol, Art. 2 (C) 1.

28. Accession Protocol, Art. 2 (A) 3.

29. Accession Protocol, Art. 2 (D) 1.

30. Zuigao Renmin Fayuan Guanyu Shenli Guoji Maoyi Xingzheng Anjian Ruogan Wenti De Guiding (Supreme People's Court Rules concerning Several Questions about Adjudication of Administrative Cases Relating to International Trade), promulgated August 27, 2002, effective October 1, 2002.

31. Confidential attorney interview #1, May 18, 2006; Confidential attorney interview #2, May 19, 2006; Confidential attorney interview #3, May 24, 2006; Confidential attorney interview #4, May 25, 2006; Confidential attorney interview #5, May 25, 2006.

32. Audra Ang, "China Pharmaceutical Appeals Viagra Ruling," Associated Press, June 20, 2006.

33. Andrew C. Mertha, "Shifting Legal and Administrative Goalposts: Chinese Bureaucracies, Foreign Actors, and the Evolution of China's Anti-Counterfeiting Enforcement Regime," in Diamant, *Engaging the Law in China,* 161–92, note 17, at 186.

34. Confidential attorney interview #2, May 19, 2006.

35. Confidential attorney interview #3, May 24, 2006.

36. Confidential attorney interview #1, May 18, 2006.

37. Confidential attorney interview #5, May 25, 2006.

38. Confidential attorney interview #6, April 4, 2007.

39. Scott D. Seligman, "Guanxi: Grease for the Wheels of China," *China Business Review,* Sept–Oct 1999, 34.

40. Thomas Gold, Doug Guthrie, and David Wank, "An Introduction to the Study of Guanxi," in *Social Connections in China: Institutions, Culture and the Changing Nature of Guanxi,* ed. Thomas Gold, Doug Guthrie, and David Wank (Cambridge 2002).

41. Quoted in Stanley Lubman, "Looking for Law in China," *Columbia Journal of Asian Law* 20, no. 1 (Fall 2006).

42. See Mayfair Mei-Hui Yang, *Gifts, Favors & Banquets: The Art of Social Relations in China* (Cornell 1994).

43. James McGregor, *One Billion Customers* (Wall Street Journal Books 2005), 110.

44. Bergsten et al., *China: the Balance Sheet,* 44.

45. "Dirty Dealing," *Economist,* August 6, 2007, 55. For an excellent analysis of government and Communist Party corruption, see Xiaobo Lu, *Cadres and Corruption: The Organizational Involution of the Chinese Communist Party* (Stanford 2000).

46. Daniel Rosen, *Behind the Open Door: Foreign Enterprises in the Chinese Marketplace* (Institute for International Economics 1999), 228.

47. David Barboza, "Ripples Keep Spreading in a Chinese Bribery Case," *New York Times,* December 1, 2006, 6.

48. Stephen Taub, "Lucent Fires Four on Bribery Suspicions," *CFO.com,* April 7, 2004, http://www.cfo.com/article.cfm/3013085 (accessed July 30, 2007).

49. BBC Monitoring Asia, "US Firm Fined 4.8m Dollars for Bribing Chinese Hospitals," May 21, 2005.

50. Confidential attorney interview #3, May 24, 2006.

51. "Shangye Huilu zhi Shengsi Tan," *Zhongguo Jingji Zhoukan,* March 13, 2006, http://news. xinhuanet.com/fortune/2006–03/13/content_4298265.htm (accessed May 24, 2007).

52. "Nankai Daxue Cheng Baoku Jiaoshou: Qiaoxiao Fan Shangye Huilu de Jingzhong," *BeiFang Wang,* March 10, 2006, http://news.enorth.com.cn/system/2006/03/10/001253027.shtml (accessed May 24, 2007).

53. Chen Feng, "China Declares War on Business Bribery," *Xinhua,* December 23, 2005, May 30, 2007, http://english.gov.cn/2005–12/23/content_135948.htm.

54. "Yangguang Caifu Zhudu Pian Zhi Fan Shangye Huilu Yantaohui Shilu," *Sina Caijing,* October 28, 2006, http://finance.sina.com.cn/hy/20061028/19053029203.shtml (accessed June 2, 2007).

55. Doug Guthrie, *China and Globalization: The Social, Economic, and Political Transformation of Chinese Society* (Routledge 2006), 109.

56. Zhu Zhe, "Stepped Up Drive against Bribery," *China Daily,* February 16, 2007, June 15, 2007, http://english.people.com.cn/200702/16/eng20070216_350597.html.

57. "China Focus: Commercial Bribery—Foreign Companies Adapt to Local Market in Wrong Way," Xinhua's China Economic Information Service, November 17, 2006, June 5, 2006, http://english.people.com.cn/200611/17/eng20061117_322599.html.

58. Confidential attorney interview #4, May 25, 2006.

59. Confidential attorney interview #3, May 24, 2006.

60. Jiang Jin, "Laodong Hetong Fa Chutai de Qianqianhuohuo," *Zhihe,* July 2, 2007.

61. Zhu Zhe, "China Adopts New Labor Rules," *China Daily,* June 30, 2007.

62. Peerenboom, *China's Long March,* 234 n.19.

63. Kevin O'Brien and Lianjiang Li, "Suing the Local State: Administrative Litigation in Rural China," in Diamant et al., *Engaging the Law in China,* 31 n.15. See Minxin Pei, "Citizens v. Mandarins: Administrative Litigation in China," *China Quarterly,* no. 152 (December 1997): 835.

64. Veron Mei-Ying Hung, "China's WTO Commitment on Independent Judicial Review."

65. Human Rights Watch, *Walking on Thin Ice: Control, Intimidation, and Harassment of Lawyers in China* (2008), http://hrw.org/reports/2008/china0408/ (accessed July 20, 2008).

66. Human Right Watch, Press Release, "China: Rights Lawyers Face Disbarment Threats," New York, May 30, 2008.

67. Comment made at conference on "Doing Business in China: The Labor and Employment Story," NYU School of Law, May 9, 2008.

68. WTO Panel Report, *China—Measures Affecting Imports of Automobile Parts,* July 18, 2008, http://www.wto.org/english/tratop_e/dispu_e/339_340_342r_e.pdf (accessed July 20, 2008).

69. Kathrin Hille and Mure Dickie, "Beijing Opens to Financial News Providers," *Financial Times,* November 14, 2008.

70. "McDonald's, KFC Probed for Wage Abuses," Associated Press, March 30, 2007; comment made at conference on "Doing Business in China: The Labor and Employment Story," NYU School of Law, May 9, 2008.

6. Conclusion: The Two Chinas of 2020

1. Merle Goldman, *From Comrade to Citizen: The Struggle for Political Rights in China* (Harvard 2005).

2. Dali L. Yang, *Remaking the Chinese Leviathan: Market Transition and the Politics of Governance in China* (Stanford 2004), 312.

3. Fareed Zakaria, *The Post-American World* (Norton 2008).

4. Author interview, May 14, 2008.

5. Author interview, May 19, 2008.

6. Tina Rosenberg, "John Kamm's Third Way," *New York Times Magazine,* March 3, 2002.

INDEX